How to Choose
Business Premises

How to Choose Business Premises

A guide for the small firm

Howard Green, Brian Chalkley and Paul Foley

Kogan
Page

Acknowledgements

We have been fortunate in being able to call upon a wide range
of specialist help in the preparation of this book. Estate agents,
planners, small business advisers, building control officers,
surveyors, and many others too numerous to mention by name,
have given up time to discuss and advise on the details of the
text. Our understanding of the small business, its property
needs and problems is based in large measure on discussions
with the small businessmen with whom we have had the pleasure
of working in recent years. In writing this book we hope we
have answered many of their questions.

First published in Great Britain in 1986
by Kogan Page Ltd, 120 Pentonville Road,
London N1 9JN

British Library Cataloguing in Publication Data

Green, Howard
    How to choose business premises: a guide
    for the small firm.
    1. Small business — Great Britain —
    Location
    I. Title   II. Chalkley, Brian
    III. Foley, Paul
    658.1'1   HD2346.G7
    ISBN 1-85091-098-7
    ISBN 1-85091-189-4 Hbk

Printed and bound in Great Britain by
Billing & Sons Limited, Worcester

Preface

This book is intended primarily for potential and practising small business owners and managers. We have deliberately avoided any precise definition of what constitutes a 'small' business, since any size boundary is inevitably subjective and arbitrary. We anticipate, however, that any firm too small to have staff specializing exclusively in property and estates matters is likely to benefit from the book. It should also be useful to small business advisers and counsellors and to teachers in educational institutions which run management courses for would-be and established entrepreneurs. In addition, we hope that the various professional groups in the property industry, such as town planners, estate agents, architects and building inspectors, may find that it helps them to appreciate the property problem from the perspective of the small business owner. These specialist professionals will not, of course, find an exhaustive coverage of their own area but they will see its position within a wider framework.

In recent years, with the accelerating interest in the small firms sector, there have been a number of publications designed to assist small businesses; there is now an established advisory literature on matters such as finance, taxation, marketing and many other facets of small business life. Remarkably, however, there is as yet no substantial text on the subject of premises. This book therefore seeks to fill a significant gap.

Contents

Chapter 1

Why Premises Matter

Surveys of small businesses have repeatedly shown property problems to be among the most serious and widespread of the difficulties facing both new and established small firms. For the would-be entrepreneur the problem may indeed be finding premises at all. For the existing firm the difficulties which can arise are more varied: it may be that the premises are in the wrong location, the wrong size, too costly, on too insecure a tenure, or so inappropriate in layout as to sabotage any chance of efficient operation.

Choosing the right premises is obviously one of the most important decisions small business owners have to make. It is also one of the most difficult. The issues are complex and can involve dealing with a bewildering array of expert professionals — solicitors, surveyors, town planners, estate agents, accountants, bank managers, architects, builders, building inspectors, fire officers, health and safety officials, insurance agents, interior designers and estate managers — all these groups and more. Knowing how and when to use them is essential if the right decisions about property are to be made and implemented effectively. Co-ordinating your dealings with this mixture of experts and getting them to do what you want is in itself a complicated exercise, but it is only one aspect of obtaining premises.

The complexity of the property problem is compounded by the fact that decisions about property and location are without parallel or precedent for many small business owners. The property problem can often look like a maze with no signposts from previous experience to offer directions or guidance.

The aim of this book is to help small business owners to choose the best possible premises and make the most effective use of them. In different chapters guidance is offered on the different types of premises available (including working from home), how to determine property needs, searching effectively, choosing the right premises, town planning and other regulations, landlords, leases and licences, managing the relocation process, and converting and organising property. Each chapter ends with a checklist of the key points which need to be considered. The final chapter contains eight brief case studies of firms with a variety of different property and relocation experiences.

Despite this breadth of coverage no book of this kind can claim to be exhaustive but, where appropriate, information is given on how to obtain further knowledge or guidance on particular issues and problems. In addition, there are appendices containing useful addresses and details of areas of special government assistance.

No attempt is made to impose a rigid system of decision procedures and policies which all small firms should adopt. There will always be a diversity of small business needs and circumstances; there is no one single solution or set of pre-scriptions. Although the ideas put forward will need to be adapted to each individual's situation, they do provide a framework for action. They are intended to provoke thought, planning and informed decision-making so that problems can be antici-pated and pitfalls averted. Ultimately, of course, it is the small business owners themselves who must make their own property judgements. Such decisions will be greatly improved if they are approached in a judicious and enlightened way.

People setting up or running small businesses are notoriously busy and hard-pressed. Faced with the prospect of investing time and money in reading a sizeable book they may need to be reminded how important the right place is to business success, so our text begins by itemising ten good reasons why premises matter and why consulting this guide should prove worthwhile:

1. Your choice of geographical location can have a major impact on your firm's prospects and profitability. For retailers in particular the choice of location is absolutely crucial in determining levels of turnover and market potential. But for virtually all businesses, location will influence the cost and ease of many day-to-day operations such as access to customers and contacts with suppliers. The extent of local competition, opportunities for developing new markets, ease of obtaining suitable staff and the speed with which you can get essential components or services will all be affected by your location. Certain kinds of government grants and financial support are also dependent on your location: for example, being in an Assisted Area, an Enterprise Zone or an Industrial or Commercial Improvement Area can bring considerable financial benefits.

2. The physical characteristics of your property, such as its size and layout, will also condition your patterns of work and productivity. Too little space imposes limitations on your business: too much space is wasteful because you are paying for something you are not using. Inappropriate layouts will hamper efficiency, lead to countless irritations, cramp your style and ambition and may even be dangerous. Although some layout problems can be overcome by careful adaptation and reorganisation of premises, there are obviously limits to what can be achieved in a difficult building.

3. You will spend many hours working in your premises: if the physical conditions are wrong your energy and enthusiasm can soon be eroded. Small businessmen have a wide range of responsibilities, work exceptionally long hours and face the anxieties of knowing that their livelihood depends directly on their firm's success. These pressures are quite sufficient without the additional stresses and strains of difficult and unpleasant surroundings. It is important therefore, within the resources available, to devote time, thought and energy to producing a comfortable and satisfying physical environment. Some individuals can tolerate grime, cold and dilapidation more easily than others but once you employ other people, environmental considerations are bound to increase in importance. Indeed, there are certain statutory conditions which have to be met. A dreary or unpleasant working environment will make it difficult to attract and retain staff. In particular, it is your best qualified and most valuable employees who will find it easiest to obtain other posts and who are least likely to put up with dismal surroundings.

4. The view which customers have of your business will be greatly influenced by the quality of your accommodation: premises and their condition create an image for any company. This is especially important if large numbers of customers visit the premises. In this case you will need at the very least an attractive and comfortable reception space. If clients are also likely to inspect the production process or work area, the whole environment will need to look clean and well-organised. If premises look uncared for customers may well infer that insufficient care will also be given to the products or services they will purchase. In the client's mind, professionalism and shoddy premises are not easily reconciled.

5. For firms buying premises the financial sums involved are

11

likely to dwarf virtually all other commercial transactions. Such momentous decisions merit painstaking consideration. You will need to weigh carefully the estimated return on the property against the likely return on investing the same capital in other ways. You will also need to ensure that the site chosen makes sense both as a place to run your business and as a property investment in its own right. In addition to using the property as a workplace and perhaps as loan security, you will probably at a later stage want to sell it at a profit. Alternatively, on retirement you may lease out the premises and derive income from it. Property transactions are a way of making money and can be every bit as lucrative as running your own business.

6. The majority of small businesses, of course, rent rather than purchase premises. But even here substantial sums can be involved in buying and selling leases. Rental outgoings (when added to rates, heating, lighting, maintenance and other property costs) can represent a sizeable element in any balance sheet and one which is a continuing rather than a once-only drain on your resources. Moreoever, whereas spending on other items can be quickly adjusted to match the state of trade, the only way of reducing rental costs is to find and move to cheaper premises. This cannot be accomplished overnight. In the short term, rental costs are therefore fixed and inflexible.

7. In the property field making mistakes on technical matters such as planning permission, building regulations or the small print on leases can cost you a lot of money and trouble. The repairs clauses in leases, for example, may involve you in considerable unexpected expenditure if you are not properly prepared. You may prefer to place these technical questions in the hands of specialist advisers but it is certainly useful to have at least an outline knowledge of what is involved and the dangers to be avoided.

8. Moving premises is a major upheaval which affects virtually every aspect of a firm's operation. It has to be undertaken while trying to keep the business running with minimum disruption to customers. Faced with this surge of demands on your time and expertise, particularly careful planning is essential to minimise mistakes and omissions. If properly managed, relocation can be much more than a change of address – it can be an opportunity to galvanise your business and to rethink and modernise your activities.

9. Moving to the wrong place will bring many more problems than opportunities. These may soon require you to move again, imposing another round of disruption, cost and management headaches. Selecting a property is rather like choosing a spouse — you are allowed to change your mind later but to do so is often troublesome and expensive. It is better to get it right first time.

10. As outlined earlier, searching for, evaluating and obtaining suitable premises can be a complex and time-consuming process and one in which you are unlikely to be really expert or experienced. These difficulties are compounded by the serious shortage, until recently at least, of most types of small business accommodation. Property companies have not generally been interested in building new small premises while town planners have substantially reduced the stock of old small premises through redevelopment schemes and strict land-use zoning. In recent years, however, the situation has eased, particularly for modern factory units between 1,000 and 5,000 square feet. In every sector of the small business property market the relationship between supply and demand now shows considerable local diversity; much depends on where you are and precisely what you want. None the less, in all cases good advice and a carefully worked out strategy are essential for success.

Chapter 2

Working from Home

Given the problems, complexity and costs of finding suitable business accommodation, it is sensible to begin by asking yourself: Do I really need business premises at all? In practice, many small firms start life in the lounge, spare-room, cellar or garage of their owner-manager's home. This is especially common among firms providing services which do not involve heavy equipment or materials. Businesses such as insurance brokers, child-minders, chimney sweeps, artists, typing agencies, accountants, architects, decorators and carpenters can readily operate from home.

Advantages

In addition to avoiding the problems and frustrations of looking for premises, working from home offers the more important and lasting advantage of saving money. You pay for only one set of housing or accommodation expenses rather than two. These savings can be considerable because by the time you have paid the rent, rates, insurance, electricity and telephone charges and perhaps decoration and maintenance costs, even the smallest workshop or office is likely to cost well over £1,000 a year. This is money which could be invested directly in the business.

Working from home can save time as well as money. The hours spent each week in commuting to and from your business premises could be spent more profitably in managing and building up your business. You will also save on the other costs of commuting — petrol, wear and tear on the car and on yourself. You will start the day fresh and finish without the prospect of sitting in traffic jams on the way home. Avoiding commuting is especially advantageous for the individual who is still working for someone else during the day and for whom the thought of heading off from home again in the evening to a distant workshop or office is not at all inviting. In these circumstances time is particularly precious and commuting even more wasteful.

Having the job and the tools to hand without the need to travel is also especially beneficial for those in creative or artistic professions. When the mood is right and inspiration strikes, everything you need is immediately available.

One final advantage of working from home is the enhanced possibility of using your family to assist with running the business. A spouse who is prepared to deal with telephone enquiries when you are out or help with correspondence, typing and other secretarial tasks, can provide valuable (and unpaid!) assistance. The same level of support may not be feasible if you are operating away from home.

In itemising the benefits of home operation it is worth remembering that for many people there is no alternative: if they do not run their business from home, they do not run a business at all. For many disabled people, for example, home is the only place possible. More generally, family commitments can in effect tie people to the house. For those bringing up young families or looking after elderly or sick relatives, working at home may be the only practicable way of reconciling business ambitions with their family responsibilities.

Domestic upheaval

This intermingling of business and family life, while inevitable for some, it not to everyone's taste. It can lead to domestic tensions, particularly if there is not a separate room suitable for your business operations, when large parts of the home come to resemble a workshop or office. Starting a business in this way can be like starting a marriage with the in-laws. You will need to persuade your family and friends to make allowances for the fact that your home is now your place of business. Even with their goodwill your family life is bound to be affected. There may be machinery in the hallway or papers and files on the dining room table, the telephone will ring day and night and customers will call at mealtimes or, by arriving early, effectively convert the living room into a waiting room. In addition, because the job is always immediately at hand you will continually be tempted to do extra bits and pieces and your spouse and children may soon get neglected. You will need to be strict with yourself if you are to retain the encouragement and support of your family. They must be allies, not victims.

Will the business suffer?

In the same way that the home-run business can harm your family, equally you need to ensure that your business does not fall victim to domestic pressures. Doing extra daily chores, shopping, home repairs and looking after the children are the pitfalls of being available at home. A solid day's work can become impossible as your business struggles for priority against the incessant demands of domestic life. Parents seeking to develop a part-time business while also bringing up children are especially vulnerable to interruptions. Ideally, you should try to set aside a period each day exclusively for the business and treat this time exactly as if you were going out to work. Alternatively, if the job has to fit around your domestic commitments, you may need to review your daily routine to allow more space for business activities.

Despite all these interruptions and pressures, those accustomed to working in a noisy factory or busy office may find working at home comparatively tranquil, especially those with no family commitments. Indeed, the home environment with its comfortable chairs, television, newspapers and drinks cabinet may offer too many relaxing diversions. Home operation requires real self-discipline. By comparison, having special business premises breeds productivity simply because the environment conditions you for work.

Your environment will also convey a message to your customers. Working from home can create the impression of a firm operating at the very margins of profitability. Some potential clients may infer that the business is unreliable and could cease trading at any time: others might feel that, without the benefit of proper premises, you may not do a professional job. For clients who seem concerned by such matters it may be worth pointing out that some of the most respected groups in British society 'live on the business', including farmers, parish priests and the Prime Minister!

Change of use

Another problem of operating from home is that you might infringe town planning regulations by making what is called a 'material change in the use of land'. The attitude of the local authority planning department to home-based firms depends on the extent to which they harm the local environment. Businesses which do not generate much traffic, do not use noisy machinery and do not annoy the neighbours, will not normally require planning permission. Other more troublesome kinds of firm will be expected to apply for planning permission which might well be refused. In the middle ground (between the Avon lady and the panel beater) decisions are inevitably subjective and may appear somewhat subtle and arbitrary. For example, permission is not normally required to use the spare room for bed and breakfast accommodation but would be needed to open a guest-house.

Generally, local authorities have over the years become more sympathetic to the needs of small firms and certainly this is the advice given to local authorities in the government's recent white paper 'Lifting the Burden' (July 1985, Cmnd 9571). Even so, many small businesses, fearful of what the planners might say, deliberately choose to operate outside the planning system. With reasonable care, tact and good relations with your neighbours, you may remain undetected for months or even years. If and when you are discovered you should apply for planning permission and if turned down, you can consider an appeal to the Department of the Environment. These procedures should normally postpone for several months the time when you are forced to cease operations, giving you ample breathing space in which to find alternative accommodation. Further details on how to apply for planning permission and make appeals are given in Chapter 7.

One particular kind of environmental regulation which you should take account of is the control of advertisements. Without proper premises, your business is just a house like any other. Advertising your presence is therefore crucial but it may get you into difficulties with the local authority. A large conspicuous sign may, in their view, strike a discordant note in an otherwise residential area. A condition of planning approval for your business might be tight limitations on the nature and scale of any on-site advertisements. Small brass plates would obviously be acceptable; flashing neon signs would not. Of course, if you are deliberately operating outside the planning system, any form of advertising (even a card in the local shop window) might give the game away.

In addition to the planning regulations, there are a number of other technical and financial matters which home-based firms need to consider. For example, if you have a mortgage you should notify the building society or bank. They are unlikely to object, but if they arrange your house insurance they may

17

need to adjust the policy. Using the dining room as an office may incur no extra insurance penalty but if your business increases the risk of fire or theft (through increased numbers of visitors) then both your home and your home contents policies may need to be changed.

Home-owners should also consult their property deeds to ensure that they do not forbid business use. Leaseholders should check the terms of their lease and tenants should notify their landlords. Council house tenants should seek permission from the local authority housing department, but be warned that many councils do not allow non-residential uses. In the white paper 'Lifting the Burden' the government has recognised that such restrictive housing management policies can pose a serious obstacle to enterprise, and local authority attitudes to council tenants may soon begin to soften. A variety of other government regulations, dealing with matters such as hygiene, health and safety, are outlined in Chapter 7.

Rates and taxes

Finally, you should be aware of two financial aspects of working from home, namely rates and tax allowances. Your rates bill may increase slightly because you will lose what is called 'domestic relief' on the part of your home which is used for business purposes. You are not legally obliged to inform the local authority rates officer of your business operation but obviously if you apply for planning or building permission or even if you simply advertise in the local press, your covert operation may well be detected.

However, you are entitled to tax relief on that part of your rates bill which relates to your business. You can also claim tax allowance for heating, lighting, repairing and maintaining the room(s) in which you work. Strictly speaking, allowances are granted only if the room(s) is used exclusively for business purposes but in practice many Inland Revenue officials are reasonably lenient on this issue and too busy to make exhaustive checks. Working from home will not normally mean that you will have to pay capital gains tax when you sell your house, but on this and other taxation matters it is important to talk to an accountant.

Working from home does have a lot of advantages for new start-ups. By removing the cost of providing and running premises it minimises one important headache for the small business, but remember that your neighbours may not think in the same way as you do. Be aware of their views and sympathetic to any comments or complaints they may have.

Key points

- Consider whether you really need business premises.
- Could you bear the costs involved in renting and running business premises?
- Would commuting be disruptive, unduly time-consuming or expensive?
- Is there a suitable room at home?
- Could your family life survive the disruption of running your business from home?
- Might family pressures interrupt your work?
- Are you sufficiently self-disciplined to work diligently and effectively at home?
- Does your business require more prestigious accommodation or would home suffice?
- Would you infringe town planning regulations?
- Would advertising controls be a serious problem?
- Contact the building society or landlord, check the deeds or lease and amend insurance policies if necessary.
- Ask your accountant about tax relief and capital gains tax.
- Be sympathetic to the views of your neighbours.

Chapter 3

The Need to Move

Why move?

There is a wide range of considerations which may encourage you to think about moving and to start looking round for alternative premises. Some firms move because they are compelled to do so by force of circumstances: 'push factors' such as lease expiry or a sharply increased rent may leave the business with little or no choice but to relocate. Many businesses move in response to 'pull factors' and are enticed by the superior attraction of a different location offering better opportunities. The list below itemises some of the most common reasons for relocation and you may well recognise here considerations relevant to your own business.

SHORTAGE OF SPACE

As firms develop they take on more employees and purchase more equipment. This often takes place slowly and gradually so that a shortage of space is not recognised until other factors intervene: new display cabinets may not allow reasonable circulation in the shop, or there may not be enough room to store the materials to fulfil a new large order. Space shortage is the most frequent reason for moving. It is often linked to other major changes within the company, such as the manufacture of a new product or the development of new markets, both of which may have significant and immediate space requirements. If your comapny has been exceptionally successful or insufficient thought was given to future space requirements at your current site, a move to alternative premises may be the only answer to the problem.

TOO MUCH SPACE

The combination of recession and technological change has led many companies to re-evaluate their space needs. Reducing the work-force, and the use of more productive machinery, have meant that many businesses no longer require the same amounts of space. Spare space costs money, not merely in

20

terms of rentals but also in overheads such as heating, lighting and rates. As companies become more conscious of these costs they may consider moving as a way of reducing them.

INCONVENIENT BUILDING LAYOUTS

Many businesses occupy premises whose layout is not really suited to the firm's needs, being spread, for example, around different buildings or sheds or over several floors. A move may therefore be necessary to improve operational efficiency.

MOVING UP THE PREMISES LADDER

While it may not be possible to begin business in the ideal property, many firms move up the industrial or commercial property market as they develop, and can afford premises which are better located or environmentally more attractive.

COMPULSORY PURCHASE

Although less common than in the 1950s and 1960s, even today some small firms are affected by compulsory purchase orders (CPOs) associated with road building and other town planning schemes. Small firms are particularly likely to be affected because they tend to be located in older property or, in the case of shops, on main road locations. Compulsory purchase was once widely regarded as highly damaging to the displaced firms. However, a CPO can in fact prove a blessing in disguise if the opportunity is taken to rethink the business, to benefit from the compensation received and to move to better premises.

LABOUR ISSUES

Studies of business movement in the UK have suggested that labour-related problems are important reasons for movement. They identify issues such as union activity, labour shortage and labour turnover. While these are unlikely to be quite so relevant to small firms (which generally have fewer employees, better labour relations and lower turnover) a move may still be necessary to overcome skill shortages.

DEVELOPING NEW MARKETS

Many businesses move premises or set up a branch unit to take advantage of new markets in different geographical locations. For example, the shopkeeper wanting to expand his trade into another town, or the business consultant wishing to satisfy demand in another city may well set up branch shops and offices.

21

GOVERNMENT AID

A variety of government grants and incentives are now offered in different parts of the country to attract new companies to areas of high unemployment. Some of these are discussed in Chapter 6. It is possible, therefore, to make a financial gain simply by moving from one place to another. Take care, though, because in practice it is usually unwise to use government inducements as the only basis for relocation. They are best seen as a bonus.

PROPERTY VALUES

If you can move from expensive to cheaper premises without damaging your business it may well be worth while. A move may prove particularly lucrative if you own premises with redevelopment potential. The site value of well located property can be significantly higher than the value of the actual buildings, especially if planning permission can be obtained for change of use and redevelopment.

PERSONAL REASONS

While we emphasise the role of sound business reasons in making decisions, many moves are undertaken for mainly personal reasons. A pleasant environment in which to live is important to us all and is of increasing significance in business location. It is particularly important in the smaller firm where the wishes and aspirations of the individual owner play the key role. The growth of smaller businesses in rural areas such as North Yorkshire, East Anglia, and Devon and Cornwall is often attributable to these environmental and personally based reasons.

Is relocation the answer?

Despite this long list of reasons for relocation, the decision to move is of such significance that it should only be taken after careful analysis. The question must be asked whether relocation is really the answer to your problems. For example, although space difficulties are the most common reason for relocation, it may be possible to solve space problems without having to move. Perhaps your existing premises could be used more efficiently, or the building could be modified or enlarged? Could existing procedures, functions and layouts be re-thought to make space savings? (Further details about layout and design are given in Chapter 10.) Alternatively, could some work be subcontracted out or undertaken by staff working at home?

If you have sufficient space around your existing premises you may be able to build an extension. This option should not be forgotten: an extension will provide extra space without the associated problems and disruption of moving. Details of the regulations involved in extending premises are given in Chapter 7. Construction methods and builders are discussed in Chapter 11.

A careful examination of all the alternatives is needed before embarking on a move. It may also be worth considering whether establishing a branch plant could be more advantageous than a complete transfer: if you simply need more space, why not keep what you have and add to it elsewhere? Growing branches can be an excellent way of exploiting new markets while retaining continuity at the old site. On the other hand, if you are in badly organised, highly inefficient buildings, a complete move may be the answer. Certainly the branch solution is less disruptive, although it runs the risk of duplicating many costs and services and of fragmenting the management and operation of the business as a whole.

Both branch and transfer decisions will bring far-reaching changes and represent major landmarks in the firm's development. Both must be costed carefully and placed firmly within the framework of the firm's investment and business plans. Location decisions cannot be taken in isolation: they should form an integral part of a wider business strategy. Is moving a cost-effective use of resources and is the kind of move proposed a better investment than other ways in which the money could be spent? Such questions must be addressed if location decisions are to enhance the firm's overall performance and contribute to its future prosperity.

Key points

- Assess very carefully why you need to move.
- Can reorganisation or extension of your premises solve the problems?
- Would setting up a branch be more advantageous than a complete relocation?
- Take advantage of any special financial packages which may be available.

Chapter 4

The Choices Available

Sooner or later, with or without 'encouragement' from the planners, most small firms need proper business premises. Working from home may be a useful launching pad but it is not usually a lasting solution, particularly if the firm is to grow. The question therefore arises: what kinds of premises are there for small businesses? It is important to familiarise yourself with the different kinds of property available to the small business. Thorough research into the market will ensure that you match your requirements realistically against the price that you can afford to pay.

The current market position

The commercial and industrial property market has been undergoing rapid change in recent years. Undoubtedly the driving force has been a new awareness of the needs of small business and a consequent growth in public-sector provision, particularly of small factory units. In the late 1970s, the Department of Trade and Industry commissioned a survey by Coopers and Lybrand. The study (published in 1980) looked at factory premises up to 2,500 square feet and identified a shortage of suitable accommodation in this sector: 'with only minor exceptions, in current market conditions demand exceeds supply throughout the country'. It concluded that 'there is clear evidence that the shortage of premises has constrained the establishment and development of small firms'.

The Coopers and Lybrand findings attracted considerable attention and helped to lay the basis for three major subsequent initiatives:

1. *A significant relaxation of town planning controls on small businesses.* In 1980 and again in 1984 the Department of the Environment issued circulars (22/80 and 16/84) to all local authorities advising them to take a much more sympathetic approach to the needs of small firms. More

recently the 1985 white paper 'Lifting the Burden' has reinforced this advice to local authority planners.

2. *An increase in the public sector provision of small factory premises.* A wide range of government bodies are now actively engaged in this field: these include local authorities; New Town Development Corporations; the Scottish and Welsh Development Agencies; and the British Steel Corporation. English Estates also has a large portfolio of factory units. Formerly known as English Industrial Estates, this organisation operates as the building arm of the Department of Trade and Industry. It specialises in factory provision in depressed regions and recently took over the building work previously undertaken by CoSIRA (the Council for Small Industries in Rural Areas). CoSIRA is an agency of the Development Commission, a government body whose aim is to enhance the economic and social welfare of rural areas. In addition to all these government organisations there has also been a growth in units funded jointly by public and private bodies, and in the provision of units by charitable trusts.

3. *Tax incentives to encourage greater private-sector involvement in small premises* were introduced in March 1980. For three years under the Small Workshops Scheme, a 100 per cent Industrial Allowance was given for capital expenditure on the construction of workshops not exceeding 2,500 square feet.

Taken together, these three government measures have had a substantial impact. In many parts of the country there has been a distinct improvement in the market position, particularly for modern factory units over about 1,000 square feet. For smaller workshops, however, the market position remains tight in some areas. This is due in part to the success of the Enterprise Allowance Scheme and other government measures designed to encourage the creation of new small firms. The increased business birth rate obviously intensifies the demand for very small, 'starter' premises. Moreover, many small businesses are not interested in new factory units but are looking instead for older, cheaper premises. At this end of the market there are often special problems for unneighbourly businesses, as town planning controls can still seriously curtail the choices available. Small motor-car repairers, glass-cutters, scrap merchants and indeed any noisy, dangerous or unsightly enterprise may well face particular difficulties in finding accommodation. In addition there is, of course, a wide range of retailing and commercial companies looking for shop or office space: parts of the property market which lie outside the realm of recent government initiatives and in which there is relatively little public sector involvement. In these sectors, market trends are less clear-cut and much depends on the general level of economic buoyancy in each local area.

Indeed, in all sectors the stock of available premises is bound to change over time and vary from place to place. This chapter does not attempt, therefore, to provide a mass of detailed information on particular places or individual properties: such a catalogue would be enormously lengthy and rapidly out of date. A general review of the state of property markets in different areas is already available in the *Business Location Handbook* produced annually by Beacon Publications Ltd (Northampton). Instead, this chapter introduces the range of different kinds of small business premises in the United Kingdom, examples of which you may well find in your own locality.

Old, cheap industrial premises

Particularly in the inner areas of our towns and cities there is a stock of Victorian and pre-First World War properties which are generally inexpensive but often uncomfortable. The building tend to be shabby and in need of repair or redecoration and there can be problems of parking and vehicle access. These old buildings were obviously not designed or laid out for the small business, but could prove useful if your preference is for the inner city and cash is an important consideration. During the heyday of urban redevelopment in the 1960s, the planners bulldozed much of the old building stock but despite this, some inner city areas continue to act as seed-beds for new small businesses. Physically, these old properties can take many forms: part of a large, subdivided factory, space over shops in a run-down retail street, rooms in what was originally a residential dwelling, or even space in a disused church or chapel. Rents vary throughout the country but they can be as low as 40p per square foot. Although much depends on the individual property, average annual rents (excluding rates) are about £2.00 per square foot in London and between £1.00 and £1.50 in the provinces.

Certain local authorities (mainly in inner city areas) are empowered to declare Industrial and Commercial Improvement Areas in which grants may be awarded for the improvement and renovation of dilapidated premises. It is worth checking with your local authority to determine whether they have designated any such areas and under what conditions financial help might be forthcoming. Further information on how to renovate and convert premises which are at present unsuitable is provided in Chapter 11.

Refurbished premises

A second though much smaller group of properties are those old buildings which have already been modernised and converted into small units. The recession has left many parts of the country with a stock of large redundant factories unsuited to modern industrial or commercial requirements and unlikely to be used again in their present form. The strong demand for small premises has led both public and private sector developers to fund the conversion and subdivision of these redundant buildings. However, rehabilitation schemes are normally worthwhile only where the rebuilding and refurbishment work can be carried out at a cost appreciably below that required to provide an equivalent new property. In practice, costs will depend on the level of dilapidation and the extent to which the original layout requires alteration. The need to comply with modern building and fire regulations can impose additional expenditure. None the less, where costs can be kept low, rehabilitation provides a means of offering accommodation at rentals below those for new, purpose-built premises. Many of the units created in this way are of an acceptable standard, comparable to newly built premises, providing an ideal first home for the new small business.

Rehabilitated premises are most commonly found in the large conurbations. London, for example, is estimated to have about one-fifth of Britain's 'rehab' units. While it is particularly in older inner city areas that industrial decline has left the largest legacy of old redundant buildings, some rural local authorities have also invested in conversion schemes. East Devon District Council, for example, has provided 37 small units in a former army training camp at Honiton.

Rental charges for rehabilitated premises will reflect the degree of modernisation, the costs of conversion and the site's

27

geographical location. A recent survey by one of the authors revealed annual rents (excluding rates) ranging from under £1.00 per square foot in parts of Northumberland, Lancashire and West Yorkshire through to over £4.00 per square foot in Buckinghamshire and Sussex. Average rents would seem to lie between £1.50 and £2.50 per square foot.

In addition to the benefits for small businesses, refurbishment can also help to conserve buildings of historic or architectural interest. In old industrial and commercial areas, such as London's Docklands, 'rehab' schemes have been a valuable means of conserving part of the local heritage by finding new uses for old buildings. One of the best-known examples is Hope Sufferance Wharf on the south bank of the Thames in Rotherhithe. The units have normally been subject to five-year leases but the intention is to move towards a shorter-term, more flexible arrangement.

Modern factory units

Over the past ten years there has been a surge in the provision of small workshop units built to standardised designs aimed to appeal to the widest possible range of tenants. Although special tax concessions have recently encouraged greater activity among private developers, most of these units have been provided by government bodies seeking to exploit the job creating potential of the small business sector. About two-thirds of local authorities have now built small units, some in jointly funded 'partnership' arrangements with private developers. The large building programmes of many of the New Town Development Corporations are an attempt to compensate for the new towns' inevitable lack of older premises. English Estates, the building arm of the Department of Trade and Industry, has concentrated its small units programme in the towns and cities of the Assisted Areas, such as Newcastle and Liverpool, where unemployment is most severe. The Council for Small Industries in Rural Areas (CoSIRA) has focused its building on the depressed rural areas including, for example, parts of Northumberland, Cumbria, North Yorkshire and Cornwall.

Small units can take four main design forms — terraced, semi-detached, detached or flatted. Terraces are by far the most common because this arrangement lowers building costs by reducing the amount of exterior walls. This in turn helps to reduce heating and maintenance costs. Terraced premises also allow some flexibility so that the size of individual units can be changed. Detached and semi-detached units are generally confined to the larger end of the small factory market although CoSIRA factories have also often taken this form, especially when building only one or two units in a village setting. CoSIRA units are noted for their high design standards, often using local building materials to blend in with the surrounding environment. Flatted factories in which firms occupy units in a multi-storey block are rarely built today, but in the 1960s, as part of the 'high-rise' fashion, a number of local authorities invested in this form of accommodation. Often the intention was to rehouse firms displaced in urban renewal programmes. For safety and environmental reasons, noxious, heavy, noisy or dangerous trades are not appropriate for this kind of property.

Rental charges for modern units depend not only on physical layout but also on location, site services provided and the quality of the environment. Many developers now take a 'bare shell' approach with few interior fixtures or facilities being provided. In such cases rents, particularly for the first occupant, should take into account the tenant's fitting-out work or should be suspended for an agreed period while this work is done. Private developers may occasionally offer a higher standard of finish with more individualistic designs or extra features, such as separate space for office activities. Although rents (excluding rates) may reach £4.00 or £5.00 per square foot for good quality modern units on prime sites, charges between £1.30 and £3.00 are more typical.

Science parks

The concept of the science park derives from recent technological developments in industry and the resultant changes in property requirements. The aim is to provide premises of flexible design which allow a mixture of research, office and manufacturing activities. Such schemes often offer shared computer and technological services together with the stimulus of proximity to other businesses working in advanced technologies. Many science parks are associated with a nearby university whose facilities are available for use. The buildings are of a high quality, sometimes futuristic in design, and the external environment is carefully landscaped. While the preference is for producers or users of new technology, some estates, especially in the private sector, have in practice been compelled by market forces to adopt a fairly relaxed definition of 'high-tech' activities. You should not, therefore, be deterred by an undue modesty about your own firm's technological sophistication.

The university science parks have, however, remained much closer to their original objectives. An example of particular interest to small businesses is the Incubator Building at Warwick University. Financed primarily by Barclays Bank, the Incubator Building provides a range of computing and other specialist services for small and start-up 'high-tech' businesses. Unit sizes range from 340 to 2,000 square feet, with leases from six months to three years. Current rentals average £4.50 per square foot plus £1.50 rates plus a £1.00 property management charge. University facilities are charged on a 'pay-as-used' basis. The Warwick development has proved a considerable success and at the time of writing all 18 units are occupied.

Shared-service workshops

The rationale behind this kind of provision is that survival rates among small firms could be considerably improved by making available on-site a range of business advisory, secretarial and other services which small firms could not afford for their own exclusive use but which can be afforded on a collective basis. Examples of such schemes can be found in both the public and private sectors. The buildings, usually refurbished premises, are often arranged on a 'rent-a-bench' or open-plan basis with movable partitions separating the units.

The services provided vary but generally they fall into three main groups:

1. Office services, including typing, photocopying and telephone answering;
2. Property related services including items such as maintenance, heating, lighting and insurance;
3. Business services, usually taking the form of an on-hand adviser who will provide advice directly and suggest other agencies if more specialist information or guidance is required.

The main advantages of this kind of accommodation lie not only in the sharing of services but in the sharing of experience and in the mutual assistance and co-operation which a community environment can engender. The main disadvantages lie in security problems (especially in open-plan layouts) and sometimes in the general level of noise and distraction.

Shared-service developments have grown rapidly in number over recent years and most large towns now have at least one such scheme. Well-known examples include Birmingham's New Enterprise workshops, Dryden Street in Covent Garden, the Avondale workshops in Bristol, the Manor Employment Project in Sheffield, the Barnsley Enterprise Centre and the Clyde workshops in Glasgow.

Another, recently opened, workspace scheme is Enterprise Plymouth. A former Rank-Toshiba factory was purchased and converted into 92 units by Plymouth City Council. The units, separated by shoulder-high concrete partitions, each have a lockable door and range from 140 to 1,250 square feet. Rental charges vary between £5.50 and £7.20 per square foot. The rents are a composite figure and include rates, background heating and lighting, a property service and security charge and a standard business advisory charge. The only 'extras' are the individual's own telephone bill and the electricity consumed within each unit. There is no formal lease and tenants can quit at 24 hours' notice. Within the building there are typing, printing, accountancy and other services which are provided by business tenants on a commercial, 'pay-as-used' basis.

Shared space

A different kind of shared space is provided when an existing business lets or sublets part of its accommodation to another firm. For companies with semi-redundant or wholly unused space, the subdivision and renting out of part of their property can be very useful in providing additional income. Moreover, firms with spare space may be going through hard times and in need of an injection of extra cash. Sharing premises in this way can also be beneficial for the prospective tenant because it provides low-cost space, flexible in both size and tenure.

It is very difficult to estimate the amount of accommodation of this kind which is available. However, given the recession of recent years it is reasonable to assume that, particularly in the more depressed regions, there must be large amounts of under-used space capable of meeting small business needs. Further information on the subdivision and subletting of spare space is contained in Chapter 11.

Shops

Retailers, of course, are interested in different kinds of property from the predominantly manufacturing, craft and workshop premises emphasised so far. When purchasing retail premises, it is more common to buy an existing business together with the freehold or lease of the actual premises. In such cases it is important to explore the track record and future prospects of the business you are buying as well as the merits of the property. Examining past trading accounts is therefore essential. Small shops tend to sell for the value of the property with fixtures, fittings and stock, plus goodwill (a crude estimate of the reputation of the business, usually valued at between one and two years' profit).

Some retail premises also have associated living accommodation in a flat or maisonette above the shop; this may have direct access to the shop floor. Living literally on top of the business can be claustrophobic. It is tempting to pop down and check the stock or tidy displays; psychologically you may never escape the business world. On the other hand, living over the shop is usually cheaper and more convenient than having a separate home and business and will certainly help to improve security.

In terms of location, retail outlets can be classified into three main groups:

1. *Town centres.* Here the volume of turnover per unit area is at its peak. The majority of shops are selling comparison goods (eg clothing) where customers check on alternative products for style, quality and price before making a purchase. A range of banking, commercial and transport services are close at hand. Another advantage is that the physical fabric of the buildings, their interior design and levels of finish tend to be of high quality. This is particularly true of the new enclosed shopping malls (eg Eldon Square in Newcastle and Brent Cross in North London) with their modern decor and controlled environmental conditions. By contrast, on the margins of the town centre and lining the roads leading out, there is often a stock of older, less glossy shops trading in a different market situation. This is the retail equivalent of the old, inner-city industrial premises outlined earlier.

2. *District high streets.* These operate as 'mini town centres'

but serve a local neighbourhood rather than the whole town. In addition to outlets selling comparison goods, there is an increased role for convenience shopping (everyday grocery and household items). The quality of the buildings, their interior finish and the products sold usually reflect the social class and income level of the population in the surrounding area.

3. *Local stores.* Whether these take the form of a parade of four to five outlets or a more isolated corner store, their function is to provide convenience goods for the immediate locality. The shops, once again, reflect the social characteristics of the area they serve but their more restricted geographical catchment generally results in lower turnover and less well finished premises. A particular variant of the local store is the village shop. This can offer obvious social and environmental attractions but, as with other local stores, their number has been affected by the increased ownership of cars, fridges and freezers and by the related rise of superstores and hypermarkets.

Within each of these main retail groups, individual premises will vary in their size, frontage length, tenure, age, condition, loading and parking facilities and in the extent of local competition. As a result, rental costs also show considerable variation. Rents for retail premises range much more widely than for the industrial and workshop premises considered earlier. This is because the success or failure of a shop is usually heavily dependent on its location. Indeed, in the words of the old maxim, there are only three requirements for success in retailing: 'location, location and location'. Prime retailing space in Central London currently costs £200.00 per square foot (excluding rates). By contrast a local corner store in a provincial city might cost as little as £5.00 per square foot. Faced with such contrasts it is obviously essential, through contact with local estate agents, to find out about rental levels in your own particular area. Further advice on property and other problems facing prospective retailers can be found in *Buying a Shop* by A St J Price. You might also find it useful to consult *How to Buy a Business* by P Farrell (both books published by Kogan Page).

Offices

All firms, including manufacturers and retailers, have to perform some office functions. The businesses considered in this section, however, are those which specialise in office activities. They are mainly concerned with the collection, storage, usage and exchange of information. Typical small business examples include solicitors, accountants, architects, insurance brokers and estate agents.

Like retailers, easy access to customers is usually a key locational consideration and the supply of office premises therefore shares some common features with the geography of retailing. In terms of location, offices can be classified into four main groups:

1. *Town centres.* The post-war years have seen a large-scale expansion of office space in the centres of our major towns and cities. The concentration of office accommodation in central locations provides advantages not only in attracting qualified staff but also in access to customers and to other offices offering related services. Much of this central office space takes the form of high-rise blocks (the concrete and glass towers of the 1960s and 1970s). In these, the units of space may well be too large and expensive for the typical small business. However, cheaper space in smaller units is often available in buildings where shops occupy the ground floor and various professional services (with similar locational needs) occupy rooms on the upper floors. Sometimes the only external evidence of their presence is the name-plate at the entrance to the building.

    In recent years town planners have become concerned at the increased incursion of ground-floor offices, especially building societies and estate agents, into retailing areas. This breaks up the continuity of the shopping frontage and introduces dead space. However, planning attitudes to the use of upper floors are generally much more relaxed.

2. *District high streets.* Although these usually have relatively few purpose-built office blocks, there is once again a stock of upper-floor accommodation. By comparison with the city centre, the geographical catchment for attracting customers is much more localised, and this will be reflected in rental levels.

3. *The suburbs.* As a result of changing patterns of communication and new developments in the transmission of data, some office companies have moved away from central

locations to cheaper premises in the suburbs. To accommodate this demand, especially around the larger cities, private developers have built modern office premises in suburban areas. Within London, for example, Croydon and Ealing are among many boroughs which now have large amounts of office space. Favoured sites are along main roads, at transport interchanges and other sites with high accessibility.

4. *Prestige, historic environments.* Some professional services, in particular solicitors, like to advertise the antiquity and respectability of their business by obtaining a prestige address in an historic part of town. A limited supply of office space can therefore be found close to cathedrals and abbeys and in areas of elegant architecture and townscape. In Sheffield the offices in the Georgian houses of Paradise Square, next to the cathedral, provide a particularly good example.

Office rents are highly sensitive to location and there are striking geographical variations. Prime office space in the City of London can cost about £40.00 per square foot (excluding rates). For similar modern premises in Croydon, Ealing or other suburban areas figures of about £10.00 per square foot are typical. However, all such costs are likely to exceed the budgets of most small firms, which tend therefore to occupy older, 'secondary' premises. A room or two over a high street shop in a provincial town may be only £2.00 per square foot, or even less in some northern towns. These steep variations underline the need to get to know your local property market.

Rents and costs

It is important to emphasise a few key points about rents and costs. A cautionary word is needed about rents quoted by some estate agents — these can be misleading. An enticingly low cost per square foot may reflect a large area of virtually unusable space, so you may end up paying over the odds for the space you can actually use. You must enquire fully into what you will get for your money. Does the figure quoted include rates? Are there any other supplementary or 'service' charges? Rates alone normally add between 15 and 25 per cent to a property's cost. You can apply for a rate reduction to the local authority ratings office but large reductions are rare. Service charges, particularly in shared-service workshops, can be even more expensive. All these various extras can more than double the rent.

Rents per unit area vary with the size of the premises being offered. Larger premises provide 'scale economies' and so on a square foot basis tend to be a little cheaper. Costs also tend to be lower in the public sector. There has been increasing pressure for local authorities and other government bodies to operate in a more commercial manner. Many public sector bodies see their main goal as encouraging business and employment rather than making money from buildings. Public sector rents may therefore involve an overt or hidden element of subsidy. For example, particularly for start-up businesses, there may be reduced rents for the first few months as a means of helping the firm to get established.

In calculating property costs do remember that rented premises may involve purchasing an existing lease. The price will depend on the property and on the next rent review date. The payment for the lease is therefore essentially 'key money' which secures your right to the premises and your obligation to pay the rent. In depressed areas it is not unknown for the lease to be considered more of a burden than an asset and for the 'vendor' to pay the 'purchaser' for taking it off his hands. In the property trade this is known as 'reverse premium'.

Given that few small businesses can afford to buy freeholds, this chapter has presented costs in terms of rentals. However, for the fortunate few contemplating ownership it is worth pointing out that the same factors which shape rentals also shape purchase costs and there are equally steep variations, especially for shops and offices. Generally speaking, freehold costs in all sectors are about ten times the annual rental charge.

As part of the government's drive towards privatisation many public sector agencies are being encouraged to sell off their factory premises. For estate management and environmental reasons, terraced units (the most common form) are still not normally available for purchase, but where public-sector detached units are on sale you just might get a bargain. This is especially true of high quality units, like those offered by CoSIRA, whose building costs in a depressed area might considerably exceed the commercial selling price. However, public sector practice is closely controlled and monitored and the best opportunities for bargain hunting usually lie with private landlords, especially those who need a quick sale. Whatever a property's theoretical book value, in practice the market value is as low as you can persuade the owner to accept.

Key points

- Review the various kinds of small business premises and decide which is the most suitable for you:
    - Old cheap industrial premises (most abundant in the inner cities: renovation grants may be available).
    - Refurbished premises (variable levels of modernisation).
    - Modern factory units (can now be found in almost all areas).
    - Science parks (they do not all insist on the highest technological credentials).
    - Shared-service workshops (a more communal life-style).
    - Other shared space (using another firm's spare floor space).
    - Shops: town centres, district high streets, local stores.
    - Offices: town centres, district high streets, the suburbs, historic environments.

- The precise mix of property types varies from place to place: get to know the local situation.

- Generally the market is tightest for very small premises (under 750 square feet) and for businesses which might be thought harmful to the local environment.

- Costs vary most in the retailing and office sectors.

- Rent subsidies or concessions are most likely in public sector factory premises.

- Rents quoted by estate agents and vendors may or may not cover rates and supplementary service charges: be sure to check.

Chapter 5

Searching for Premises

Deciding what you want

Now that you are aware of the different types of small business premises, it is time to consider precisely what sort of property you need. A clear set of objectives will help you search more efficiently. If you know what you are looking for, you will not waste time visiting premises which do not meet your requirements. A written checklist will also make it easier to evaluate the sites you inspect. Because it is unlikely that you will find exactly what you want, the search will inevitably develop into a series of compromises and trade-offs between the pros and cons of particular premises, but by preparing a checklist you can undertake the process of compromise in a more structured way.

While you are preparing a checklist of priorities it is also worth talking to people in your search area who have a knowledge of property matters and the state of the local property market. Although you will accumulate knowledge over time, this process can be accelerated by discussions with estate agents, local businessmen, small firms' advisers (such as the Department of Employment's Small Firms Centres) and local authority industrial development officers. Check to establish whether there is an Enterprise Agency in your area. An up-to-date list of agencies can be obtained from Business in the Community (see Appendix 1 for the address). These bodies aim to encourage and support small businesses; through their network of local contacts they might have some useful ideas about your checklist and the prospects of finding what you want locally. Many Enterprise Agencies keep lists of property suitable for small businesses.

If you are starting in business for the first time, outside advice can be particularly helpful. The best people to approach are other small business owners who have recently started trading. Compare your checklist of requirements with their experiences. Ideally you should talk to people in a similar line of business to your own, although some will be wary about giving 'tips' and 'trade secrets' if you are viewed as a potential new competitor.

Among well established companies, and particularly those with some experience of moving, there is a temptation not to give relocation the careful planning it merits. An extreme example of this is a recent case in Suffolk where a small business owner wanting to expand signed a three-year lease on a newly completed 1,500 square foot unit built by the local authority. When he visited them to collect the keys they were more than surprised to find that he had never even been to the unit and he had to ask for a map to find out where it was. This kind of casual approach is not to be recommended! Even if you are already in business it is likely that there will be aspects of the intended move with which you are unfamiliar. Guidance from other businesses, advisory services and local authorities is free and often invaluable.

It is usually better if you approach these groups or individuals after you have developed at least a provisional checklist of property requirements. This allows them to offer you more specific advice and it helps to show that you are planning carefully and are serious in your request for assistance.

Given that every business will obviously have its own individual requirements, no two checklists will have exactly the same detailed content, but at a broad level there are certain items which virtually all checklists will need to consider. These are discussed below.

LOCATION
The importance of locational considerations varies enormously between different businesses. Location matters most if your customers come to you to collect goods or services. Retailers are therefore especially sensitive to location.

What then makes a good retail location? Two key ingredients are a high pedestrian flow and a large local resident population. A site in a prosperous shopping centre or street is advantageous because you can benefit from the success of other businesses in attracting shoppers to the area. If, however, the area is in decline and you detect that other local traders are in difficulties, you may also be damaged by their lack of success. Although a direct rival in the same trade next door can be a competitive threat (especially in a small centre) retailers tend to sink or swim together. Obviously, sites in prosperous centres are expensive and for this reason people new to the retail trade and with limited resources often begin in secondary areas or in corner stores. They hope to build up the business, gain experience and then move on to something better. In judging the relative merits of alternative sites it can be useful to count the number of shoppers in the area and to walk round the neighbourhood to identify the extent of competition and whether the local residents are in the right income bracket for the goods you intend to sell. If you carry out a pedestrian count you should repeat the exercise at different times of the day and week.

Shops selling specialist goods, such as musical instruments or fishing tackle, do not usually require a prime location with high pedestrian flow. They are less dependent on passing trade and impulse buying. Most customers requiring specialist goods are willing to make a special journey and travel longer distances to get what they want. For this type of shop a sufficiently large local population is the key geographical consideration. From this it should not be implied that any retail premises will suffice. Specialist shops still need to be accessible and good parking facilities can be advantageous.

The importance of location for office activities depends upon the precise nature of the business. For activities such as accountancy, where customers visit the premises, the locational needs will be broadly similar to those of specialist shops. Parking may well be a major consideration. If the office function is simply processing forms or invoicing, with little direct customer contact, a more out of the way location could be considered.

For other kinds of business the importance of location will depend mainly on the frequency and urgency of contacts with customers and suppliers. The more frequently such contacts are made and the greater the involvement with 'rush jobs', the more significance attaches to a location with high accessibility. This may mean a site in or near the centre of town or alternatively a suburban site on a major road or near an important road junction. Communication facilities, including public transport, also become increasingly significant the more people you employ.

Whatever your business there are advantages in places which enjoy high 'imageability' and are well-known to the public. Sites which are off the beaten track will fail to provide exposure and may deter customers who fear they might have trouble finding you. Sites next to well-known landmarks such as churches or pubs are definitely to be preferred.

In evaluating possible locations you need to consider not only the area as it is now but as it may be in the future. Talking to local people can provide useful impressions of how the place is changing. In addition, officials in the local authority planning department may provide a more objective account, including information on whether the local population is increasing or declining and how (if at all) the area is changing in terms of social class. Above all they will be able to inform you whether there are any major planning proposals, such as roads, housing or redevelopment schemes which are likely to affect the area in the future. Local searches by a solicitor prior to buying or leasing property will also reveal any relevant council plans.

Finally, on a wider note, you should consider the possibility of obtaining government assistance if you locate in certain specified areas. In order to encourage new jobs in places experiencing severe unemployment, loans, grants, subsidies and other financial inducements may be offered. The geographical extent of these areas is highly variable. For example, Enterprise Zones are often only a few hundred acres in size and Industrial and Commercial Improvement Areas are even smaller, whereas Assisted Areas cover whole regions with populations running into millions. Whether you can use these opportunities will obviously depend on how far you are prepared to move and whether these areas are attractive in other ways. Certainly it would be unwise to gear your whole locational strategy around the pursuit of government aid, but this can be a decisive factor when two places are otherwise finely balanced. Further information on this subject is available in Chapter 6.

SIZE

Although most firms start trading on a modest scale, business premises should normally allow for some reserve space. This will avoid the problems and frustrations of operating in a cramped environment. It will also enable you to cope with steady expansion or a sudden upturn in demand without having to move premises. Relocation is costly, disruptive and time-consuming. Having space available for expansion can avoid these problems. How much reserve space you require depends on how rapidly your business is expected to grow. Be realistic and do not over-burden yourself with large areas of redundant floor space which you are paying for but never likely to use. Remember you will be paying rent, rates and other overheads such as heating, lighting and insurance for space which is not earning you money.

If you have not run a business before, or even if you have, you may not be very familiar with floor area measurements. When premises are advertised their size is usually expressed in square feet. It may be useful to familiarise yourself with what 500, 1,000 or 2,000 square feet actually means in terms of floor area. Try measuring your lounge, garage or garden and use this as a guide towards specifying your firm's floor space needs in square feet.

Recent business surveys suggest that the average floor space per employee in manufacturing is about 300 to 400 square feet. Such average figures, however, disguise enormous variations. One manager in Huddersfield who knew he had excess space was surprised to find that he had no less than 8,000 square feet per employee. Another manager who wanted to move to larger premises had a floor space density of one worker for every 80 square feet. Relative to manufacturing, office-oriented businesses tend to need rather less space, averaging about 200 square feet per employee. By contrast, wholesale and warehousing businesses are often more space extensive and figures of 600 to 700 square feet are common. These survey figures are only a very rough guide to your floor space requirements: different firms have different needs. If you think you will require, or already have, more space than the figures mentioned above, check your calculations again. Although excess space may be essential if you are planning to expand, it may also be a luxury you can ill-afford if your plans are not realised.

TENURE
Nearly all small firms want to rent rather than buy property. This is especially true in the formative years of business development when capital is particularly limited. Your firm's future outlook may in any case be too uncertain to justify a major investment in premises. This unpredictability generally leads to a preference for short-term leases of, for example, three or six months. If your business proves strikingly successful you may want to move to larger premises; if your business fails you will want to move out and stop paying the rent. Either way, you are likely to benefit from short-term arrangements. (Further details on leases are provided in Chapter 8.)

COSTS

How much you can afford to spend is, of course, another major item in your checklist. Your ability to pay for premises will play a key role in determining the kind of premises you should be looking for. Try expressing your likely property costs as a proportion of your expected turnover and you will clarify how sensitive your business is to differences in accommodation costs. This will help to indicate whether you can afford to pay a little extra for more inviting surroundings. On this, as on all important financial questions, you should consult your accountant and seek good advice, particularly if you are contemplating buying a property. If you will need to borrow money get a preliminary indication from banks and financial institutions on how much they might be prepared to lend you. (Further information on sources of finance is given in Chapter 6.)

In practice, as explained above, renting is the usual pattern for small firms. Rent charges, particularly on small premises, are variable and you can encounter large price differences for premises of broadly similar size and quality. It is extremely important to search around and get a good feel for your local market before making any final decisions. In this way you will be able to gauge what is a reasonable rental for the kind of property you are considering.

The way in which prices are quoted can vary considerably. Normally only rents are quoted; occasionally the rateable value will also be given. It is important to note that this is not the actual rates payable — these will depend on the local authority's rate in the pound. If you are considering premises with associated access to secretarial, cleaning and other services, it is advisable to find out whether these items are included in the price of the premises. If they are, find out, if possible, how much of the rent is in fact a fee for these additional services. There is a tendency for some developers to overcharge for them. Also make sure that the rent quoted is a standard price and not an introductory offer. In many parts of the country, particularly in private sector developments, rents are increasingly negotiable. Reductions of 20 and 25 per cent on quoted rates are not unheard of, while some landlords are offering initial rent-free periods. In this latter case, make sure that you are not paying for this concession with a higher overall rental during the full period of the lease.

Rents are usually expressed as a price per square foot per annum. It may help if you translate such statistics into costs per week or month since many small businesses find this is a more immediate and meaningful figure.

CONDITION

Although many small businesses look for cheaper, older premises as a means of cutting overheads (and sometimes rightly so), before adopting this approach you should ask yourself these questions:

- Will shabby premises damage the firm's image with potential clients?

- Will I need pleasant working conditions for employees?

- Will I work happily and effectively in difficult or uncongenial surroundings?

In addressing these questions you will be reminded of the various ways in which cheap accommodation can cost you a lot, in terms of both money and job satisfaction. It is essential to keep your overhead costs within your budget but you may end up paying a heavy price for 'cheap' premises. On the other hand some cheaper, older property on the market at present can offer very good accommodation, appropriate for the new start-up business. There is considerable variation throughout the country; search carefully in your local area.

LAYOUT

By thinking through the intended day-to-day operations of your business (including production, storage, office and sales functions) you should develop an insight into the property layout and shape most suited to your needs. Will you, for example, require a separate office or storage room? Where will you meet prospective clients? If you use heavy machinery or materials, floor loadings can also be an important consideration. In such cases a ground floor may be essential. Ground-level premises also have the advantages of accessibility and of being more visible to members of the public passing by. This can be useful in attracting customers.

PARKING AND ACCESS

Try to assess the nature and volume of traffic your business will generate. Large lorries may find access difficult in narrow lanes and cul-de-sacs. Estimate how many of your visitors will call by car. How much parking space will you need? A particular site may be able to accommodate all the car parking you require. If this is not the case you may be able to make use of local on-street parking. If you have to use on-street parking make sure there is plenty of space and that congestion and parking problems will not damage your trade. Be sure to visit any prospective property during mid-week working hours and at peak times in order to assess parking problems.

Sources of property information

Once you have formulated a checklist of property and locational requirements you can begin the actual search. Make sure at the outset that you get a map of the area(s) under consideration. It could save a lot of time. Many of you will know from experience in hunting for houses just how difficult and dispiriting property searches can be and how great can be the difference between an agent's glowing description and the reality you encounter on inspection. The search process will therefore probably result in a downward adjustment of your requirements and an increased willingness to make compromises.

Six methods of searching for premises are given below. Those likely to be most useful are given first but much depends on the particular kind of property you require.

LOCAL AUTHORITIES

Many local authority planning, employment or estates departments now keep a premises register for small businesses. They tend to concentrate on industrial properties but some also have lists of shop and office accommodation. The local authority acts as a central information bank by compiling lists of available premises both in the public and private sectors. The lists are regularly updated and though they inevitably fall short of being absolutely comprehensive they are often the single best source of information.

ESTATE AGENTS

These are an obvious search channel. Most of the smaller agencies deal exclusively with residential properties and you will need to concentrate on the larger ones and those which specialise in commercial and industrial premises. Many of the larger agencies also operate as business transfer agents. They will sell an existing trading business together with its premises. Some estate agents have a tendency to promote only their most expensive premises; since their commission is based on first year rents this is hardly surprising. Make sure you ask them about cheaper property if this is what you want. Remember that it is normally the vendor not the purchaser who employs and pays for an estate agent. Ideally, you should call in at the agent's office (you will get better service this way) but if you do enquire in writing just ask for details of vacant premises and do not make any statements which might be construed as commissioning the agent; otherwise he just might try to charge you for his services. If you live a long way from your area of search it may be more convenient to employ an agent to undertake the search on your behalf.

WALKING OR DRIVING AROUND THE APPROPRIATE AREA(S)

This can sometimes bring to light vacant properties which have not been formally advertised. For some properties, the only advertising undertaken is by billboards outside the premises. Touring the local area and making enquiries may reveal a firm which is contracting and not using part of its building. This could provide you with the space you need and at the same time provide extra (rental) income for the 'host' firm.

PERSONAL CONTACTS

Your contacts in the business world can also be useful. By telling as many people as possible of your accommodation needs you can have a large army of 'spies' vigilant on your behalf. The members of any local small firms' organization can be particularly helpful in this respect. It is also useful to discuss your requirements with all your contacts. Their experience may help to highlight items or locations which you have not considered on your checklist. They may also warn you about particular premises which look like bargains but which for various reasons would be detrimental to any business acquiring them. Do not be afraid to ask for other people's advice as this could prevent you from making expensive mistakes.

LOCAL NEWSPAPERS

The local press usually have property sections which you can use either to scan the premises listed or to advertise your own requirements. Most newspapers have a particular issue during the week which is generally accepted as the 'industrial/commercial property day', although it may be worth looking at the properties vacant column throughout the week. If you are inserting an advertisement be sure to choose the property day.

OTHER SOURCES OF ADVICE

Other groups which might be helpful include CoSIRA, English Estates, Enterprise Agencies and the Department of Employment Small Firms Service. (Addresses for all these are in Appendix 1.) The Small Firms Service provides advisory and counselling services on many facets of small business management and, as suggested earlier, you might find it helpful to discuss your accommodation preferences and problems with them. The Small Firms Service and the other business advisory services do not function as estate agents, and while you might get some good general advice you are less likely to learn of particular vacant properties.

Key points

- Draw up a checklist of requirements.

- What size of premises will you need?

- What type of tenure: freehold or leasehold? If leasehold, what length of lease?

- How much can you afford for premises?

- What quality of working conditions do you require?

- Decide what type of layout your business requires.

- How much traffic will your business generate? What are your parking and access needs?

- Decide which kind of location best meets your requirements.

- Take into account the possibility of government aid in certain areas.

- When you have prepared a complete checklist discuss it with business advisers and friends.

- In searching for premises use as many different information sources as possible.

- Contact local authority planning, employment or estates departments.

- Visit estate agents. Ask them about cheaper property if they are not actively promoting it.

- Walk or drive round the local area. Some property is only advertised by billboards.

- Use the local newspapers either to advertise or to check the premises-to-let column

- Use family, friends and business contacts to help your search.

- Get in touch with any small firms' advisory bodies operating in your area.

Chapter 6

Financing and Selecting a Property

Previous chapters have offered guidance on how to assess what type of property you need and how to go about finding it. But these carefully laid plans will of course come to nothing unless you have the money to turn your ambitions into reality. For some small businesses the financial costs of new premises may be less troublesome than the extra work and worry involved in relocation. Indeed, if you are selling your own premises and moving into rented accommodation, the capital benefit will pay not only for the move but also for a host of other useful investments. For most firms premises will not be a boost but a drain on resources, and finance will be needed to meet the various costs incurred. Particularly if you are hoping to buy premises (or to take out a long lease) it is important to contact an accountant. You will need good advice on what you can afford and how much you can or should borrow. Although only a minority of small firms are involved in buying freeholds or long leases, for those who do, these commitments are among the largest financial decisions they are likely to make. For that reason this chapter focuses on the various sources of funds which are available to finance your premises, as well as offering guidance on the final stages of actual property selection.

The two processes of finding a property and obtaining the money to pay for it are closely interwoven and tend to proceed in tandem. Certainly for those intending to finance premises by means of a loan, obtaining the necessary capital is the central task. Once you have drawn up a preliminary checklist of your property requirements (and before you have a particular building in mind) it is important to look into the availability of funds. Exploratory discussions with an accountant and with funding agencies will test the feasibility of your plans, and may suggest changes to your ideas and adjustments to your checklist.

Most firms requiring finance will have to borrow from a commercial lender of one kind or another. The next section will introduce you to the most commonly used sources of finance. The reader requiring more detail is advised to consult a

HOW TO CHOOSE BUSINESS PREMISES

specialist text on this subject. A particularly useful example is Clive Woodcock's *Raising Finance: the Guardian Guide for the Small Business* published by Kogan Page (2nd edition 1985).

Sources of finance

HIGH STREET BANKS
The high street banks are the most obvious source of loans. Any local branch should be able to provide further details and itemise the information they will require from you before finance will be granted. In general, banks are the most appropriate source of funds but if you do use them always contact more than one because their interests rates and terms vary. In recent years the commercial banks have become much more flexible and positive in their lending policies to small firms. They used to lend only relatively modest amounts to small businesses and usually over time periods of less than five years; now they are increasingly competitive. Under the right circumstances most banks are prepared to lend for up to 20 years. They will consider lending almost any sum of money provided that suitable security is available.

MERCHANT BANKS
Merchant banks provide long-term finance and capital for growing businesses. Unlike the high street banks they do not provide overdrafts or bridging loans. The major part of their business is with term loans and mortgages of between five and twenty-five years. With adequate security there is no real limit to the amount they will lend, but their minimum is usually around £50,000. Because of the larger amounts they deal with, merchant banks tend to lend only to companies or individuals with a proven track record. They usually insist on a thorough look through your accounts. Your track record will determine how flexible the merchant banks will be. They will usually lend up to 75-80 per cent of the property's value. One drawback of many merchant banks is that they often lend only on an equity basis, taking shares in your company in return for the capital they loan.

INVESTORS IN INDUSTRY PLC
Investors in Industry (previously known as ICFC) is a merchant bank type of organisation owned by a consortium of high street banks and the Bank of England. Their head office is at

50

91 Waterloo Road, London SE1 8XP; tel: 01-928 7822. Their particular interest, as their name suggests, is in industrial lending. Investors in Industry pride themselves on their assistance to small private companies. In 1985 two-thirds (£227m) of their new investment went to small businesses and over half of the year's total investments were in amounts of £100,000 or less. Their emphasis on lending to smaller industrial companies can sometimes make them more responsive than merchant banks who have a much wider-ranging investment policy.

BUILDING SOCIETIES
Some building societies, predominantly the smaller ones, will give mortgages to purchase industrial and commercial property. Indeed, many societies are keen to expand their lending in this area, so this may be a growing area in their future activity. Some of the larger societies offer private purpose loans which, as their name suggests, can be used for any purpose including the purchase of premises for your business. The type of security required is variable, but if a large enough proportion of your household mortgage is 'paid off' this may satisfy their requirements. You can use a mortgage broker to identify the building society whose terms best meet your needs. The broker's service should be free. Avoid paying any 'facility fees'.

LOCAL AUTHORITY SCHEMES
Many local authorities, anxious to encourage local economic development and employment growth, offer loans and in some cases grants to help small businesses move or purchase premises. As the availability and terms of these grants and loans varies between authorities you should contact your local authority's industrial or economic development officer for information.

Presenting your case to a financial organisation

This section outlines the basic steps you should take when trying to arrange finance from one of the organisations discussed above. In practice the details will vary according to the nature of your business, the sum required and the organisation you approach. The procedures set out below are those which commonly apply when borrowing sums of about £5,000 to £50,000. If you are seeking a smaller amount the procedures may be shorter; if you wish to borrow more you may have to prepare a more detailed case.

51

Your initial visit to a financial organisation, before you have a particular property in mind, will be brief and purely exploratory. The aim is simply to make contact and to alert them to the fact that, unless they reject your ideas at the outset, you intend to return when a property has been found. Once you have identified the property you want a second visit should be arranged as soon as possible because speed may be essential if you are bidding against other interested businesses. You should prepare a brief document (three or four pages) giving basic information about your business, the property (use the estate agent's handout), the amount you wish to borrow and the preferred method of repayment. It also helps to have a written letter of recommendation from your accountant, a professional business adviser or, if appropriate, from your bank manager. At this meeting you will be 'sounded out' in a fairly general way. It is unlikely that you will be asked any highly specific or penetrating questions about your firm's financial or cash flow position, but be ready with some basic facts and figures just in case. If they are satisfied with your initial ideas and interested in your proposition they will invite you back for another interview and a more thorough assessment.

For this final interview you will need a much more detailed document which, because of its essentially financial nature, is best prepared with the help of an accountant. It should include the following information:

1. Details of your business (your product, markets etc) together with any sales or publicity material.
2. Details of the property in which you are interested (use the estate agent's brief).
3. The amount of finance you require and the preferred methods of borrowing and repayment.
4. An historical analysis of your firm's finances (generally three years' minimum).
5. The most recent trading figures and audited accounts.
6. A forecast of cash flow and your trading position.
7. Details (if appropriate) of your management team and their expertise.
8. Your company's major shareholders (if any).
9. Your current banking arrangements.
10. Any assets which are available as security.

Preparing a document of this nature will take time. If you are confident that you want to move and that you have a strong case for financial support, you can prepare the document even before you have found a suitable property. Details of the actual premises can then be added later. Preparing the document so far in advance can be a gamble especially if it becomes clear later that they are not interested in your proposal, but most financial organisations will be impressed by these early preparations made without them having to specify exactly what is required. It will certainly enhance their estimation of your management capabilities.

During the final meeting you will be asked questions about the accuracy and realism of your facts and forecasts. If your knowledge of accounts is not strong enough to withstand a barrage of questions, take your accountant with you. This should ensure a professional presentation, but it does not mean that you can sit back and leave everything to your accountant. You too will need to know the document 'inside-out'. Be confident and positive. Their personal impressions of you will be important; it is often a gut feeling about the applicant which sways the final decision. Good health, integrity, logic, imagination and experience are key attributes that most investment managers will be looking for in a client.

A word of caution is appropriate here. Most lending agencies can differentiate between an accountant's plan and a small firm's plan. They will be looking for what you want to do, aided by your financial advisers, not what your advisers would like you to do. After all, it is you as proprietor or owner-manager who will be implementing the decision.

The appointment of a surveyor to examine a property and ensure its value and future well-being is usually undertaken near the end of the financial negotiations. In this way surveyors are not employed until the lending organisation is fairly confident they will lend money for the purchase of the premises.

Either during or soon after the final meeting you will be told whether or not they are willing to lend you the money. If you do not succeed with one organisation, take heart — there are plenty more you can approach. Try to learn the lessons of your failure so that you can prepare a stronger case next time. However, if you get a series of rejections you may need to rethink your proposals or even to reconsider the whole idea of relocation.

The major sources of grants and preferential loans

Although most firms needing finance will have to borrow some money from a commercial lender, numerous kinds of government assistance are also available. Some are directed exclusively at small businesses and others are more widely available. This section outlines some of the most commonly used sources which are relevant to property. It focuses on the assistance you may be given if your property is located in certain geographical areas. This is a complex field and if you need more detail, a comprehensive account is given in *Industrial Aids in the UK 1985: a businessman's guide* by Mishka Bienkowski and Kevin Allen, published by the Centre for the Study of Public Policy, University of Strathclyde, Glasgow. If you think you might be eligible for a particular form of assistance contact the organisation concerned.

ASSISTED AREAS
Some areas of the country with particular economic problems or high levels of unemployment have been designated by central government as 'Assisted Areas'. This makes them eligible for regional policy assistance. Government regional policy divides the assisted areas into two groups. The first group comprises the development areas and here both regional development grants and regional selective assistance are available. In the second group, the intermediate areas (where unemployment is generally rather less severe), only regional selective assistance is available.

Regional development grants take the form of tax-free contributions towards capital expenditure, including premises. Generally the grants are intended for the manufacturing industry, but certain management, service, research and technical activities are also eligible. The rate of capital grant is set at 15 per cent, subject to a limit of £10,000 for each new job created (though this ceiling is not normally enforced for firms with less than 200 employees). Alternatively, labour-intensive projects can claim £3,000 for each job the investment creates. For every approved application both the capital and the job grants will be calculated and firms will automatically be paid whichever is the greater.

Regional selective assistance is discretionary but can be provided for projects which provide or safeguard jobs in any part of the assisted areas. It has to be demonstrated that the project would not take place on the basis proposed without government assistance. Relocation schemes are eligible, but only if there is an increase in jobs. The amount of assistance is negotiated on a case-by-case basis and is fixed at the minimum sum needed to bring about the benefits associated with the project. Regional selective assistance can be awarded in conjunction with a regional development grant but eligible expenditure is then assessed net of this grant.

For further information on regional policy and enquiries on eligibility you should contact your regional office of the Department of Trade and Industry (addresses in Appendix 1). In Wales and Scotland you should contact the Welsh and Scottish Offices respectively (addresses in Appendix 1). A list of the development and intermediate areas is given in Appendix 2.

ENGLISH ESTATES
Although English Estates' prime concern is the direct provision of industrial and commercial premises in the assisted areas (and in certain rural locations), they can also arrange mortgages with financial institutions at favourable interest rates. For further details contact your nearest English Estates office (addresses in Appendix 1).

BRITISH TECHNOLOGY GROUP
The British Technology Group was established to promote innovation and investment in British industry. Within the English assisted areas the Group has a wider role than its normal technological focus. It helps all companies which have growth potential and can improve their efficiency by modernisation or rationalisation. This can include money to finance premises if this is part of an overall improvement programme. For further details contact the British Technology Group at one of the addresses shown in Appendix 1.

COUNCIL FOR SMALL INDUSTRIES IN RURAL AREAS
The Council for Small Industries in Rural Areas (CoSIRA) aims to improve the prosperity of small businesses in certain rural areas of England. Similar services are offered by the small business divisions of the Scottish and Welsh Development Agencies and the Local Enterprise Development Unit (LEDU) in Northern Ireland. Loans for building capital are available to small firms in the manufacturing, service and tourism sectors. Loans are usually for up to 50 per cent of project costs, from a minimum of £250 to a maximum of £75,000. Addresses are in Appendix 1.

ENTERPRISE ZONES

As part of an experimental project, the government has designated 25 Enterprise Zones in various parts of the United Kingdom. The aim is to increase economic activity by offering financial and tax incentives and by relaxing town planning and other administrative controls. The most important of these measures for most small businesses is the exemption from paying rates on their premises. The locations and contact addresses for the Enterprise Zones are given in Appendix 2.

INNER-CITY AREAS

Certain urban areas, designated under the Inner Urban Areas Act 1978, are eligible for loans and grants to assist with property issues. These areas are listed in Appendix 2. Under Section 5 of the Act companies in Industrial and Commercial Improvement Areas are eligible for grants and loans for the conversion, improvement, modification or extension of industrial or commercial buildings. Section 10 assistance is restricted to special areas; this offers grants towards the cost of rents paid by firms taking leases for premises intended for industrial or commercial use. Section 11 of the Act provides grants for small businesses in special areas to assist with interest payments on loans (from virtually any source) for land and/or buildings.

All areas designated by the Act are also eligible for Urban Development Grants (UDGs). This is a flexible scheme providing financial assistance for projects developed by local authorities in partnership with local businesses. Projects can include industrial and commercial building or redevelopment schemes. For further information on all these urban and inner-city schemes you should contact your local authority.

BRITISH STEEL CORPORATION (INDUSTRY) LTD

BSC Industry aims to assist economic growth in 17 areas where steel closures have occurred. Most of these areas are also eligible for low interest European Coal and Steel Community funds and many receive aid because they have been designated as development or intermediate areas. In each of its 17 areas BSC Industry offers assistance with finding premises (often rent or rate free), technical advice, and guidance on preparing applications for local authority or government assistance. For further details contact BSC Industry at NLA Tower, 13 Addiscombe Road, Croydon CR9 3JH.

NCB ENTERPRISE LTD

NCB Enterprise Ltd was set up by the National Coal Board in 1985 to ensure that new jobs were created in areas where pits have closed. The company is currently supported by funding of £20m. It can provide loans to small businesses which may be used for the purchase of premises. Alternatively, it can provide sites and premises for the small firm. A full list of NCB Enterprise Ltd area contacts is given in Appendix 1.

EUROPEAN COMMUNITY FUNDS

The European Investment Bank provides fixed-interest, medium-term loans to firms investing in projects which create or safeguard jobs in the assisted areas. The European Coal and Steel Community provides loans for companies located in areas where there have been coal or steel plant closures. Loans are for manufacturing and service companies which undertake projects that could, potentially at least, employ redundant coal and steel workers (though they do not have to do so in practice). Loans are for up to 50 per cent of the fixed asset costs of a project. Some grants are also available from the European Regional Development Fund. For further details about European money in England, contact your regional office of the Department of Trade and Industry (addresses in Appendix 1). In Wales, contact the Welsh Development Agency at Pearl House, Greyfriars Road, Cardiff CF1 3XF. In Scotland, contact the Industry Department for Scotland, Alhambra House, 45 Waterloo Street, Glasgow G2 6AT.

INLAND REVENUE

Many of the costs associated with setting up a new business or relocating an existing one are eligible for corporate tax relief. This includes expenses related to the disturbance of your employees.

It is possible to defer capital gains tax incurred when selling your existing premises if the proceeds are invested in constructing new accommodation.

It is also possible to obtain tax relief for capital expenditure incurred in the construction, conversion or purchase of new buildings to be used for productive, manufacturing or processing trades. The Industrial Building Allowance Scheme for Small Workshops has now been phased out; however, a writing down allowance of 4 per cent is still available. These Industrial Building Allowances are claimed by the property owner, though it may be possible by negotiation for an incoming tenant to persuade the landlord to 'share' the benefit. The allowance is payable only if the unit is let to particular types of enterprise, essentially manufacturers. For further details contact your local office of the Board of Inland Revenue. For units not exceeding 1,250 square feet, contact the Small Firms Service of the Department of Employment (addresses in Appendix 1).

Deciding on a property

It is only when you have confirmed at least in principle that finance will be available to fund your new premises that you should begin a detailed assessment of alternatives. Looking over new industrial or commercial property is rather like looking round a new house: there are certain things to look out for and check. Although you are strongly advised to take professional advice from a chartered surveyor about the property you finally choose (and if you are borrowing money to purchase a property, your bankers will insist on a full survey), you can save yourself money by carrying out initial investigations yourself. You can spot obvious problems without recourse to a surveyor. A telephone call to the planning and building control officers, for example, will quickly confirm the use for which the building has approval. Further details of these issues are given in Chapter 7.

It is worth visiting the property more than once at different times and on different days of the week. You will be surprised how a clear sunny day can brighten up even the most gloomy property. Remember that the vendor or landlord may have spruced it up so that you are seeing it at its best. If you are doubtful about the premises or the landlord, try to find out why the previous occupier left. If the landlord is not helpful ask nearby businesses.

It is a good idea to make a list of all the items you want to look at. It is all to easy to become engaged in conversation with an eager vendor or his agent and miss many important points. How many times have you asked yourself where the kitchen door was located or which bedrooms had fitted furniture, on your return from looking over a new house? In putting together such a list you should consider some or all of the following.

STRUCTURE
Before finally deciding on a property make an initial assess-

ment of its structural stability by looking for signs of weakness. Cracks or bulges in walls and surfaces out of plumb may indicate a building needing expensive underpinning. They may on the other hand reflect local settlement just after the building was erected. Roof timbers should show no sign of weakening especially where they enter the walls. Check that the floors are in good condition. In multi-storey property floors should be capable of taking the loads you want to place on them and stairways should be sound. Look for damp and condensation; it may be caused simply by a blocked gutter or may be due to more serious problems. Check the roof carefully. Asbestos and felt roofs can be very expensive to replace.

Remember that many older properties often look dilapidated and yet are very sound structurally; a thorough clean and a coat of paint may be all that is required to transform them into ideal workspaces.

LAYOUT

Is the layout suitable for your business? Try to work out where all your main items of equipment will go. If your business involves dust or noise is it possible to create a space where office work can be done in peace and safety?

SERVICES

Check that the premises have all the services installed which you will need. Heating can be very costly so you should check both the system itself and the fuel costs. If in any doubt ask to see the previous year's bills. Look carefully at the electricity supply and wiring. Is the property separately metered? Does it have three-phase electricity? Is the wiring in good condition? In older property look out for modern 13 amp sockets. The older 5 amp and 15 amp round sockets almost certainly indicate the need for rewiring.

Whatever business you are engaged in you should look around the vicinity of the property. What businesses are there nearby? Will they create nuisance? Are there parking restrictions which might inhibit customers? Does the area feel right for your business activity?

Many people's final judgement is based largely on intuition. They accept the first suitable property visited without resorting to complex decision-making. Others will draw up a shortlist of properties and take the best. The approach you adopt will depend on how urgently you require the property, the number of suitable premises available, and the current demand for property. Some business owners with more methodical minds use scoring systems which allow them to compare all the checklist elements for each property. Obviously these elements will not be of equal importance and to account for these differences they should be weighted. Simply distribute 100 points between them so that each checklist item gets the number of marks relative to its importance. For the properties visited each factor is then marked out of ten. The total score for a particular property is derived by multiplying each item's score by its weighting, and then adding up all the scores. A simplified example using only four checklist factors at two locations is shown below.

A simple property assessment

Factor	Weight	Property A		Property B	
		Factor score (out of 10)	Overall score	Factor score (out of 10)	Overall score
Location	35	7	245(7x35)	9	315(9x35)
Size	30	8	240(8x30)	7	210(7x30)
Condition	20	5	100(5x20)	9	180(9x20)
Layout	15	8	120(8x15)	5	75(5x15)
TOTAL	100	TOTAL	705	TOTAL	780

When you have finally decided on the premises, you should engage a chartered surveyor to undertake a structural survey. This is important even if you are leasing rather than buying the property as the survey will indicate the state of repair of the property, for which you may well be responsible. You should specify that you want a full structural survey as opposed to a valuation survey. It might also be necessary to specify the detail required in the structural survey. Many surveyors, for example, will not undertake a full investigation of the roof or ascertain floor loadings unless specifically requested.

The cost of a structural survey varies considerably and it is wise to obtain two or three quotations. As your bank or lending agency will commission a survey for valuation purposes you may find it useful to use the same practice for your own structural survey. In this way you may save money as you will otherwise be paying, directly or indirectly, for the bank's valuation too. The bank will normally only survey the property when they have decided that your application for money is worthy of their support.

The information contained in the surveyor's report will be particularly valuable when it comes to negotiating terms for the purchase or lease of the property. The report itself will indicate the implications of any findings on the asking price or rental. Defects in the fabric of the building will be good reason to negotiate the asking price downwards. Such defects may also necessitate exclusion clauses being included in a full insuring and repairing lease agreement. The opportunities for negotiation will clearly vary between different landlords and vendors. If you are renting a standard terraced unit on a local authority industrial estate, the rent will be fixed. It is unlikely that the local authority would permit tenants to pay different rents for exactly the same property. You may, however, be able to negotiate an introductory offer or reduce the price of any fixtures and fittings. Remember that if you are taking on an existing lease, its detailed terms, including the rent, will already be specified. In this case the scope for negotiation may be confined to the cost of obtaining the lease (ie the premium of 'key money').

After you have decided

SOLICITORS
Once you have found a property you definitely want, you should consult a solicitor. Do not sign anything straight away. Every year a number of businesses lease, and in some cases, buy, property which they are later unable to use. This is because the regulations described in the next chapter do not allow them to carry out their particular business activity in the chosen property. It is up to you, usually through your solicitor, to check these conditions. Indeed, it is one of the solicitor's main roles to ensure that the building can legally be used for the purposes you intend and that it meets town planning and other regulations. The solicitor's searches with the local authority should also reveal whether the property will be affected by future town planning proposals such as urban redevelopment or road building. The solicitor's other main duties are to 'investigate the title' (to ensure that the person selling actually owns the property or lease) and to make arrangements for the preparation and exchange of contracts. In all these matters

your solicitor should be seeking to protect your interests and to ensure that there are no 'hidden' snags or problems, for example, easements — drains underneath your property which could be accessed by others. For this reason many businessmen prefer to use solicitors who are willing to visit premises and look for these types of problem.

In addition to dealing with strictly legal matters, many solicitors perform a variety of other tasks. They may, for example, appoint a surveyor and interpret the report; they may also advise on finance and negotiations over price. You can, of course, bargain with the vendor directly and not even use the solicitors as a post-box, but you should at least keep them abreast of what is going on so there is no danger of 'crossed wires'. It is for you to judge how much weight to attach to the solicitors' non-legal advice, but if they strongly disagree with your proposed course of action it is probably worth making further enquiries and getting a second opinion.

When choosing a solicitor (if you do not already have one you use regularly) you should seek guidance from business contacts and friends whose judgement you trust. Make sure that their recommendation is based on first-hand experience rather than hearsay or casual gossip. Before making a commitment you should get estimates from two or three solicitors. The average cost of conveyancing for a 1,000 square foot unit is between £300 and £500, but charges are highly variable. Although it is important to shop around it is not always wise to use the solicitors with the lowest quote; if this is overrun, they will in effect be working for you for nothing and this may lower their motivation and diligence. You will need to weigh the strength of recommendations alongside cost in making your decision.

One final and important aspect of these legal transactions is that prospective tenants are usually expected to pay the landlord's legal costs for administering your tenancy. It is worth including a clause in your lease or in negotiations prior to moving, that these costs be 'fair and reasonable'. In most cases your landlord's costs will be similar to your own, so in calculating the expense of a move to a rented accommodation you should double your own costs to take this into account.

This additional burden may be enough to tempt you into saving on one set of fees by doing your own conveyancing. In recent years this idea has attracted considerable interest in the domestic field. However, given the pressures on small business managers, relatively few will have the time to become sufficiently expert to 'do it yourself'. When there is so much at stake and so many other things to worry about, you may well decide to leave it to the professionals.

SATISFYING THE LANDLORD

When choosing a property and negotiating the terms of its hire, you are obviously seeking the best possible package you can get. Do remember, however, that just as you are looking for suitable premises, so landlords (or estate agents acting for them) are looking for suitable tenants. They may well subject you to some degree of screening or vetting to check whether you are likely to make a good tenant. Although in recent years the market has swung in the tenant's favour (and landlords have had to become less choosy), they still retain the right of veto. If you really want a particular property it is important to understand the kind of tenant the landlord wants so that you can present yourself in the best possible light.

All landlords share a basic preference for tenants who will pay the rent on time, who will not go bust and who will not damage the property or cause a nuisance to other tenants nearby. Beyond these minimum specifications, tenant selection practices vary substantially between different agencies and individuals. CoSIRA, for example, prefer firms with job-creation potential and if possible a rural or craft 'flavour'. Their screening procedures are rigorous and may include a full history of the firm, details of your business experience, balance sheets and cash flow projections. By contrast, the English Estates' small units unconnected with CoSIRA are managed rather differently. Here there is less concern over the nature of the business and the financial investigation is often more cursory (for example, taking up references). Among local authorities there is a wide range of different practices but generally, as a public sector agency, they will give preference to firms likely to create new jobs. Some authorities also prefer manufacturing to service sector businesses: industry is often seen as basic to an area's economic well-being. Local authority decisions are usually taken by an estates sub-committee of the council which will usually confirm the recommendations of the estates department officers.

In the private sector there are many different kinds of developers and landlords and there is, as a result, a considerable diversity of approach. In contrast to government bodies, for private landlords the property's profitability is the key target and hence ability to pay the rent is what really counts; less concern is given to the type of business and its capacity to generate jobs and reduce unemployment. Screening may be undertaken by estate agents or directly by the developer or landlord. In the case of premises affected by Industrial Building Allowances and Regional Development Grants, the landlord will be looking for 'qualifying tenants'. In this instance the type of business is important.

Key points

- If relocation will require financial help, start looking into the availability of funds at an early stage.

- Review the various forms of government assistance and determine if you might be eligible.

- Contact a variety of financial sources: rates and terms vary.

- Be positive, professional and well prepared when dealing with financial organisations.

- Remember that many of the costs of obtaining premises are eligible for tax relief.

- When visiting premises prepare a checklist of things to look for.

- Try to determine why the previous occupier left.

- Think through your layout arrangements: how would your activities fit into these spaces?

- Consider using a points system to compare properties.

- Negotiate on price and other items.

- In choosing surveyors and solicitors shop around.

- Make sure there are no legal or other impediments to your intended use of the property.

- Present yourself in a good light to prospective landlords and their agents.

Chapter 7

Planning, Building and Health Regulations

Introduction

While obtaining your property may be a very simple exercise, it is more likely to be protracted and to involve considerable negotiations. As part of that process you may need to contact a variety of people with an official interest in what you are doing. Various pieces of legislation and official bodies may have to be consulted to ensure that you will be able to use the property for your business. Other activities will also require the approval of these groups. Building an extension to your current property and, in some cases, internal building or restructuring work may require approval. Many of the groups will have to be contacted if subdivision or conversion of a property is contemplated (see Chapter 11). Each group of officials will examine your proposals from a different viewpoint. The main groups who may need to be consulted or involved are:

- Town planning officers.
- Building control officers.
- Environmental health officers.
- Fire officers.
- Health and Safety Executive.

This may seem daunting but some of the consultation and approvals may be done automatically for you. The planning authority, for example, may consult environmental health officers in the process of giving planning approval. All local authority departments are likely to be located in the same building, making the process of consultation a little easier.

The following sections analyse what each group of officials will be looking for when they consider your proposals, and give some hints on the approach you should take.

Town planning

Planning controls have become a highly emotive issue in the last few years. However, the problems they pose can normally be overcome if certain general principles are followed. Two very useful publications prepared by the Department of the Environment are available free from all local planning departments. The first, 'Planning Permission — A Guide for Industry', gives a detailed account of how to obtain planning permission, and the second, 'The Small Firm and the Planners', answers questions specifically relevant to small businesses.

It is quite possible to submit a planning application without hiring a specialist adviser. The local authority planners are there to help and in many cases some guidance from them will be all that is needed to secure a successful application. If, however, you feel nervous of the form-filling and bureaucracy you can ask your solicitor to deal with them. If you are required to submit a number of scale drawings and plans of the property you may need an architect or surveyor to prepare them. Only in really complex cases will it be worth hiring a planning consultant. Names and addresses of consultants can be obtained from Yellow Pages or from the Royal Town Planning Institute, 26 Portland Place, London W1N 4BE. Equally rarely, legal advice may be needed and there are legal practices which specialise in planning law. In all cases, shop around as there is considerable variation in the fees charged. In the overwhelming majority of cases you will not need a battery of experts. Like many tasks which are unfamiliar, gaining planning permission may appear daunting at first sight but generally speaking, it is relatively straightforward. The notes below offer a simple guide to the main questions you will need to consider.

IS PLANNING PERMISSION REQUIRED?
Planning permission is needed for most construction and building work. However, there are some exceptions including:

- *Some temporary buildings and small extensions.* For example, an industrial property may be extended by 25 per cent of its existing volume up to a maximum of 1,000 cubic metres.
- *Internal alterations, painting and decorating.*
- *Property demolition*, except in the case of listed buildings or premises in Conservation Areas.

Planning permission is required for a 'material change' in the property's use. If, however, the building was last used for the same kind of purpose as you intend, then permission is not normally needed. To determine technically whether there is a material change of use, planners refer to the Use Classes Order which classifies business activities into a number of different groups. It is only when the property would move from one class to another that permission is needed. This sounds reasonably straightforward and usually is, but just occasionally there may be some uncertainty about which class a particular business should be placed in. If there is any doubt contact the local planning department. Examples of the more relevant use classes are:

Class I	Use as a shop (except for those selling hot food, tripe, pets, cats' meat and motor vehicles).
Class II	Use as an office.
Class III	Use as a light industrial building.
Class IV	Use as a general industrial building.
Classes V to IX	Are for special industrial groups involving more dangerous or obnoxious industrial processes such as alkali works, smelting or plating metals, processes involving burning, industrial recovery processes (refining oils, recovering rubber and other chemicals), working with animal products (fat melting, glue making, bone grinding etc).
Class X	Use as a wholesale warehouse or repository.
Class XI	Use as a guest house or hotel.
Class XVII	Use for activities such as a dance hall, Turkish bath or sports hall.

The Use Classes Order is at present under review so it is important to check the current position with your local planning authority. Remarkable as it may seem, it may be necessary to establish the 'use' that a building has permission for at present. It is one thing to be carrying out a particular business activity and quite another to have established permission to do so! In such cases the permitted use will have to be established. This is called a 'Section 53 (of the 1971 Town and Country Planning Act) determination'.

WHICH ORGANISATIONS SHOULD BE CONTACTED?
In most cases the district council planning department should be contacted for permission or further advice. In some areas, however, permission is either not required or is obtained from a different organisation, and these instances are:

- *Enterprise Zones.* Twenty-five Enterprise Zones have

been established throughout the country: the contact addresses are listed in Appendix 2. Most developments are granted automatic planning permission (as long as broad guidelines are observed). There are, however, one or two exceptions and some types of development may not be permitted. Where planning permission is needed, it is usually given within 14 days. Other types of environmental and safety controls, for example building regulations (see below), still operate in Enterprise Zones and the relevant approvals will be needed.

- *New towns.* Here, planning matters do not normally come under the control of the local authority. The New Town Development Corporation is the appropriate body to contact.
- *Urban Development Areas.* In London and Merseyside Docklands, planning matters are the responsibility of the London Dockland Development Corporation and Merseyside Development Corporation, to whom all applications should be directed.
- *Special Planning Zones.* These will be rather like Enterprise Zones. In these areas, once the planning authority has specified the types of activity it will allow, appropriate developments can take place without the need for planning permission. As this concept is new, ask your planning authority if they have as yet designated Special Planning Zones.

In Scotland and Northern Ireland a slightly different planning system operates. Northern Ireland, for example, is divided into eight divisions for planning purposes; enquiries and applications should be directed to the divisional planning officer. The system in Scotland is distinctive largely because of the different administrative system. In the Central Region, Fife, Grampian, Lothian, Tayside and Strathclyde, planning is divided between regional and district authorities. It is the district authority that should be approached. In Borders, Dumfries and Galloway, and Highland Regions, there are no district planning authorities and the regions deal with the control of development. On the islands, the Island Area Authorities deal with development control.

HOW ARE PLANNING APPLICATIONS MADE?
It is usually best to begin by discussing your proposals informally

with a planning department officer. Obtain a copy of the appropriate application form and seek the officer's guidance on any parts of the form which pose problems. You should discuss what the chances are of getting permission and which of the various kinds of planning application you should make. The four kinds of application are:

1. *An outline planning application.* In the case of expensive building works you may wish to avoid preparing detailed plans until you know whether you are going to get planning permission. You can therefore apply for approval in principle by submitting an outline application. Any drawings submitted at this stage are for illustrative purposes only.

2. *An application for approval of reserved matters.* Outline approval will have to be followed by a second application to clear up items of detail not previously considered. These are referred to as 'reserved matters'.

3. *A full application.* This is the type of application to be adopted if you require a change of use. A full application is also needed in order to regularise the position if development has been carried out without approval.

4. *Renewal of temporary permission or relief from conditional permission.* This type of application is usually made to verify or modify conditions imposed in a previous approval.

You do not have to own the property on which you wish to make a planning application. Normally it would be unwise to buy or lease a property without having first obtained planning permission for the use you intend. However, in some circumstances, obtaining permission before you buy or lease could push up the price of the property.

HOW ARE DECISIONS MADE?
Decisions are usually taken by a planning committee which will consist of local councillors and council officers (professional employees); the committee will usually make a decision within eight weeks of your application being submitted. In exceptional cases a decision may take longer than eight weeks but the authority must inform you in writing of any delay. Generally this only happens for major developments which require extended consultations.

Most applications are successful and you should only be turned down if the council can show strong grounds for doing so.

Such grounds might be the effects on road safety, noise, unsightliness and damage to the local environment. In recent years central government has instructed local authority planners to take a more sympathetic approach to small business applications. Circulars 22/80 and 16/84 and the recent white paper 'Lifting the Burden' have all pointed firmly in this direction, but there is still considerable discretion within the planning system and attitudes vary from one authority to another. Occasionally approval will be given, subject to certain conditions or restrictions on your mode of operation. For example, you may not be allowed to operate your business at certain times of the day or week in the interests of nearby residents.

Planning permission lapses after five years if not acted upon, so you do not have to start any work immediately. If after five years no development has been undertaken you will have to re-apply for permission which may not automatically be granted.

HOW MUCH DOES PLANNING PERMISSION COST?

Advice from local planning officers is free but actual permission costs money. For example, outline permission can cost between £53 and £1,325 depending on the size of the development. A change of use certificate costs £53. For the erection of buildings there is a sliding scale of fees (1985 rates):

- Where no new floorspace is created £27
- Up to 40 square metres of additional space £27
- Between 40 and 75 square metres of additional space £53
- For each additional 75 square metres £53 up to a maximum of £2,650

Each separate application is chargeable even though it may relate to the same property, so it is important to think carefully about the development and include everything on one application.

WHAT IF PERMISSION IS REFUSED?

The council are required to give reasons for their decision and you may be able to overcome their objections by modifying some aspects of your proposal. Alternatively, you can make an appeal to the Secretary of State. The Department of the Environment has produced a free booklet, 'Planning Appeals —

a Guide', which is available free from the Department of the Environment, Planning Inspectorate, Tollgate House, Houlton Street, Bristol BS2 9DJ.

Six months are allowed from the date of the decision in which to appeal. An appeal does not have to be expensive; it need not involve a Public Inquiry and can be undertaken in writing. It is always worth considering, as about 30 per cent of appeals are successful.

Finally, remember that planning decisions are enforceable by law and although many authorities will take a sympathetic view of an oversight, enforcement can lead to the demolition of buildings or cessation of unapproved uses.

Building regulations

Building regulations are, in certain respects, the most important statutory requirement to be considered if you are thinking about undertaking any development work on property. Do not be tempted to undertake any works without consultation and, if necessary, approval from the building control department. There will be very few occasions on which building control approval is not needed even if you are only subdividing space. Building regulations are administered by the building control department of your district council. The basic aim of the regulations is to ensure that buildings are safe and structurally capable of withstanding the intended types of use.

THE NEED FOR APPROVAL

Broadly speaking there are two kinds of development which require building regulations approval. These are:

- *Building works.* Most forms of building work will require approval. For example, applications are needed for structural alterations, the erection of internal partitioning and the installation of toilets and other such fittings.
- *Change of use.* Even if no building work is involved, a change of use from one 'purpose group' to another will need approval. These 'purpose groups' are not the same as the planners' 'Use Classes', see page 67. Examples of some of the most relevant groups are:

    iv   office
    v   shop
    vi   factory
    vii assembly
    viii storage.

71

APPLICATIONS AND DECISIONS

Although in theory it has been possible for a variety of qualified bodies to grant building regulations approval since November 1985, this wider system is unlikely to become fully operational for a number of years. In the immediate future make an application to your local authority building control section. Particularly where building works are involved, you will normally need an architect or surveyor to prepare the necessary drawings. In the simplest cases, however, you may get by with some free guidance from one of the building control officers. Whereas town planning decisions are normally made by elected councillors, building regulations decisions are taken by the professional officers. You should know the outcome of any application within five weeks. There is an appeals procedure which involves a representation to the Department of the Environment.

FIRE RESISTANCE

In many building regulations decisions, one of the key concerns is the spread of fire both within and between buildings. Indeed, it is common for the local authority officers to consult specialists in the Fire Service on these matters. Certain structural elements of your building will be required to reach minimum periods of fire resistance. 'Structural elements' will include beams, columns, floors, external walls, compartment walls, structures enclosing protected shafts, loadbearing walls and galleries. Minimum periods of fire resistance for the structural elements of any building in any purpose group are determined by the height, floor area and cubic capacity of the building. Fire resistance requirements tend to increase with the size (floor area and height) of the building, so a careful note should be made of these details before submitting an application. Minimum periods of fire resistance for the structural elements of a property are usually much higher for older multi-storey buildings than for single-storey buildings. This will be an important consideration if you decide to purchase property to convert and subdivide (see Chapter 11).

The requirements of building regulations can, on occasion, be relaxed if certain specifications cannot be met. Whether a relaxation is given will depend on the merits of the building itself. The provision of adequate fire fighting equipment and adequate means of escape, early warning systems and sprinkler systems can all facilitate the relaxation of certain building regulations requirements.

BUILDING REGULATIONS CHARGES

Approval for a change of use is free, but where building work is involved there is a sliding scale of fees which is based on 70 per cent of the estimated costs of the work to be undertaken. This is one of those cases where it pays not to exaggerate total cost!

The table below shows two kinds of charge, one for dealing with the plans and the other for the inspection visits. (An official will call to check that the work is being carried out properly and in accordance with the regulations. The number of such visits will vary with the scale of the development.) There is only one inspection fee. You will not be charged according to the number of visits actually made.

Examples of building regulations fees

70% of estimated cost of works	Plan fee £	On-site Inspection fee £
Under £1,000	3	9
£1,000 and under £2,000	7	21
£10,000 and under £12,000	32	96
£100,000 and under £140,000	203	609
£700,000 and under £1,000,000	945	2,835

Since 1 June 1984 all extensions and alterations have been subject to VAT at the standard rate of 15 per cent. This must be included in the estimated costs.

Building control approval lapses after three years from the date of the approval if it is not acted upon, in which case a new application has to be submitted. Although it is unlikely that the new application will be refused, some upgrading of specifications may be necessary. Changes in insulation and ventilation standards, for example, have necessitated upgradings for previously approved plans.

Environmental health

The environmental health department of the local authority is responsible for the health and physical welfare of the population. Key areas include:

- Dust, odours and fumes.
- Grit and dust from boilers and industrial processes.
- Noise (often a problem in residential areas).
- Food and food hygiene.

In the case of food, the environmental health officer will want to be sure the premises conform to the Food Hygiene (General) Regulations 1970. These lay down standards of construction, lighting, ventilation and sanitary provision. A useful guide, 'Your Guide to the Food Hygiene (General) Regulations 1970', produced by the Health Education Council is available free from the Health Education Council, 78 New Oxford Street, London WC1A 2AW, or the environmental health department in your local authority.

If you propose to do any new building or make alterations to your premises you would be well advised to consult your environmental health officer. Any suggested modifications or requirements can then be accommodated at an early stage, so avoiding possible trouble in the subsequent occupation or use of the premises.

Fire certificate

Most firms will need a Fire Certificate to confirm that the precautions taken in the building have reached a standard acceptable to the fire officer. If you have already obtained building regulations approval this should not cause a problem. Certain smaller buildings do not require a certificate but never leave the possibility in doubt! Even if the building has an existing certificate, it may be necessary to re-validate it if certain changes take place. These will include items such as:

- Any change in use as defined in the building regulations.
- Any change in the processes to be used or materials stored.
- The subdivision of the existing building to multiple use.

All buildings which require a Fire Certificate will normally require a fire alarm system, fire fighting equipment and possibly an emergency lighting system. The fire prevention officer in your area will be only too pleased to discuss the fire safety of your property. If you go to visit the fire prevention officer, take along a plan of your property. This need not be an architectural drawing but a simple sketch marking items such as doors, staircases, storage areas, fire escapes and the location of any fire fighting equipment.

A leaflet entitled 'Fire Safety for Small Businesses' is produced by the Fire Protection Association, Aldermary House, Queen Street, London EC4N 1TJ, and is available free from your local fire prevention officer or the Fire Protection Association.

Other legislation

Two other main Acts will apply to your business. These are the Health and Safety at Work Act 1974 and the Offices, Shops and Railways Premises Act 1963. There is some degree of overlap between these.

To comply with both you must ensure that employees work in a safe and comfortable environment; not too hot, cold, damp or noisy. Welfare, catering and toilet facilities must be kept clean and safe. Equipment must be properly guarded and maintained. Floors, steps, stairs, passages and gangways must be kept safe and free from obstruction.

Generally, the legislation is enforced by the Health and Safety Executive and its various inspectorates. In some cases local authority officers, including the environmental health officers and the Shops, Health and Safety Act inspectors (who are responsible for wholesale and retail trades, hotels and catering, offices and commercial activities) may be involved. Other specific legislation applies to individual places. Restaurants and cafes must be approved by a food inspector, while licences are required from the local authority for a wide range of trades such as hairdressing and ice-cream manufacture. Periodic visits are made by the inspectors, during which they assess whether your property is up to the appropriate standard. If any improvements are required the inspector will take one of two courses of action:

- He may give informal advice, either verbally or in writing, usually backed up by one of the many leaflets produced by the Executive.
- He may take formal action including improvement notices, prohibition notices and prosecution.

The inspector's approach will depend on the seriousness of the problem, other attributes of the workplace and the general responsiveness of the management. A prohibition notice can halt a process or practice until it is brought up to the appropriate standard, so the area of health and safety should be taken very seriously. Both the Health and Safety Commission and the Health and Safety Executive produce a series of excellent leaflets which address both general and specific health and safety issues. The Commission's leaflets 'Advice to the Self Employed' and 'Advice to Employers', and the Executive's leaflet 'Securing Compliance with Health and Safety Legislation at Work' are well worth reading. They are available free from one of the 21 area offices throughout the country (addresses in Appendix 1).

Key points

- Make a list of all those who may be involved in the approval of your use of the premises.
- Check with each whether:

  (a) you need their approval.
  (b) your proposals are satisfactory.

- In your approach to these officials:

  — Be adaptable and take advice
  — Do not be put off by technicalities
  — Ask for any relaxations possible
  — If necessary appeal against any unfavourable decisions
  — Make sure you get all relevant permissions before signing any contracts.

Chapter 8

Leases and Insurance

Leases

This section is obviously intended mainly for those renting property. It will, however, be of use to those who intend to convert and subdivide property (as discussed in Chapter 11) thereby becoming landlords in their own right.

If you decide to rent property and become a tenant a whole range of possibilities and constraints arise. First of all you will have to resolve the contractual relationship with your landlord. In the past the only form of arrangement was a lease. A lease stipulates the precise conditions of your tenancy. In recent years, however, a more flexible arrangement for letting commercial property, called a 'licence', has become increasingly common. The licence is particularly appropriate in properties likely to be occupied by start-up companies as it offers an 'easy in, easy out' approach to letting. It may have attached some of the same conditions as a longer-term lease, but without the longer-term commitment. Moreover, licences save money because they often avoid solicitors' fees. In spite of these advantages, the licence is still not universally popular with new companies. This may well be because it is new and little understood. Although many tenants still seem to prefer the security of a good old-fashioned lease, it is well worth investigating the possible use of a licence. Remember that a licence is not a legal interest in premises and does not formally bring protection from the Landlord and Tenant Act. Similarly the licence is not a 'valuable' interest and cannot be sold in the way that a tenant can sell a lease at a premium.

As the property market in many parts of the country is not very buoyant at present many developers are offering premises, particularly older ones, on even more informal terms. This may be a simple letter of agreement requiring one week's or one month's notice on either side, or even no formal agreement at all. Whether you opt for such terms will depend very much on the scale of your business and the level of uncertainty surrounding its future. Shorter-term agreements can be ideal if you are just setting up and testing your business skills for the first time. In all cases do remember to negotiate with the land-lord to obtain the kind of agreement and associated conditions you want. There is plenty of scope for negotiation in the small business property market; in many parts of the country a 'buyers' market' exists at present and prospective tenants have the upper hand in negotiations.

The traditional business tenancy is on a fixed-term lease of anything from three to twenty-one years' duration. It may be even longer. The lease will set out the terms which you have agreed with the landlord. Included will be the rental level, frequency of payment, date of commencement and duration of the lease. Among the other items which may be covered are rates, repairs, insurance and any estate management charges and liabilities. It is usually advisable to get a solicitor to check the details of the lease, but do shop around — solicitors' rates are becoming increasingly competitive.

Other key items to consider are discussed below.

RENT REVIEW

Rent reviews are commonly built into leases. They provide for rent increases, often on a three-, five- or seven-year basis. Review periods are negotiable and it is in the tenant's interest to keep the review period as long as possible. Ensure you know what the review process includes. Although you should always be given six months' notice before the changes come into operation, there are leases in which the review is stipulated at the outset. For example, a nine-year lease may include clauses which fix the rent at £1,000 for the first three years, £1,300 for years four to six, and £1,600 for years seven to nine. In this way you know exactly what your liabilities will be and can trade accordingly.

Negotiating or accepting future price increases for leases is exceedingly difficult because trends in the industrial and commercial property market are notoriously difficult to predict. A stipulation that increases will be in line with retail prices might seem appropriate but there are many indices other than the Retail Price Index (RPI) which could be used and which increase at different rates. Consider longer-term agreements carefully. You may end up paying above the market rate if prices decline in real terms. A shorter-term lease will always reflect prevailing market rates more accurately and ensure at the very least that you are not paying more than you need.

SUBLETTING

A clause is frequently included in leases to control the practice of subletting. This is generally to protect the landlord against undesirable tenants. These clauses, frequently referred to as covenants, can take one of two forms: an absolute covenant preventing subletting, or a qualified covenant in which subletting may take place only with the landlord's consent. Check what is involved. Also find out whether the covenant applies to all or only part of the building. Normally leases will prohibit the subletting of only part of the premises but will often permit the subletting of the whole, subject to the landlord's approval.

The extra income from subletting has helped many struggling businesses during the recession. If you are buying your lease from an out-going tenant do make sure that he is entitled to sublet the property and that the lease allows you to carry on your business. If you are taking on a sublet, make sure that the tenant has the right to create a subtenancy. A good solicitor should automatically check these items for you.

'USUAL COVENANTS'

The term 'usual covenants' is used to cover a wide range of circumstances which come within a commonly held convention. These may include:

- Payment of rent, rates and other taxes.
- Maintenance and repair of the property.
- Landlord access to examine the condition of the property.
- Repossession in the event of non-payment of rent.

Of particular importance, because of the possible expense involved, is the question of maintenance and repair. Many landlord-tenant disputes have revolved round levels of maintenance and liabilities associated with repair. For example, who is liable for the repairs of major structural defects which arise in the building during the life of the lease? These responsibilities can be extremely expensive especially in older property. It is important to minimise your liability associated with fair wear and tear. Take care to check that your insurance covers you against as many of these risks as possible and if necessary seek professional advice.

ALTERATIONS AND IMPROVEMENTS

The lease will specify any restrictions on modification to the building. While the tenant may claim compensation for any improvements made, the landlord may ask for the premises to be reinstated to their previous condition at the end of the tenancy. Make quite sure what your position will be when the tenancy ends. It might appear to be a long time away but the sum involved may be considerable. It is also important to ensure that the value you have added to the rental as a result of your improvements is not subsequently included in a rent review. It is not uncommon for a tenant to find himself paying twice for his improvements: once for the building work and once for the rent increase which this building work 'justifies'. Provided that the improvements have been made with the landlord's approval, the Landlord and Tenant Act offers protection from this double payment. If you are threatened with a rent increase which you feel is based on your improvements you should contact a valuer or solicitor.

TERMINATION OF LEASE

There are two common causes of the termination of a lease: either the occupier gives the landlord an agreed period of notice to leave, or the lease is forfeited because one or more of the terms of the agreement have been broken. The agreed period of notice will be one week for a weekly tenancy, three months for a quarterly tenancy and so on. In the case of a fixed-term lease, this will be at the end of the term. However, if you want to terminate the lease before the end of the agreed period, the landlord will decide whether to re-possess the property or not. He may hold the tenant to the terms of the lease.

It is obviously advantageous if possible to negotiate a lease which you can surrender quickly or easily assign to another business. In practice few private landlords are willing to accept surrender provisions, though conditions are easier in the public sector.

Insurance

Whether you are buying or leasing property it is vital to check your insurance liabilities. You will want to insure the contents of your premises. If you purchase the building you will also be responsible for insuring the structure. If you rent, then the premises can be insured by the landlord, tenant or both. Do not leave insurance to chance. Check the lease and discuss with the landlord who is responsible for insurance.

Commercial insurance is very similar to the domestic cover on your house and its contents. Different companies offer different packages to suit a variety or risks. You will find great variation both in the premiums charged and in the attitudes towards small businesses and particular risks. There are four broad areas of cover which you should consider:

- Property.
- Contents and work in hand.
- Public liability (business risks).
- Employers' liability.

PROPERTY

The most important cover for property is against fire risk. Most companies deal with fire cover as a separate item. Some policies include a 'loss of profits from fire' component which is well worth considering. In these policies standing charges such as rent, rates, salaries, interest payments and increased costs of working are covered, as well as loss of profits in the event of fire.

Fire cover premiums depend on the size and nature of the buildings and the trades carried on within them. Buildings with roofs made of combustible material are more expensive to insure than those of non-combustible material. If a building has a sprinkler system installed, this can reduce the premium payable by up to 50 per cent. However, insurance companies will insist on regular cleaning of nozzles, testing of water supply and maintenance of water storage tanks. Trades which have an increased fire risk (eg paint factors and welders) may have to satisfy special conditions. Different insurance companies include different trades within this category, so it is worth shopping around if your business could be classified as a special fire risk (see also page 74).

Normally, insurance of 'other perils' has to be taken in association with fire cover. However, in some circumstances, usually when leases demand it or sums insured are quite high, other perils can be covered separately. Risks which are covered in this way are similar to those in your domestic contents insurance and include storm, burst pipes, riot and explosion. If your property has large areas of display windows, it will be worth looking into additional insurance to cover this risk.

HOW TO CHOOSE BUSINESS PREMISES

CONTENTS

Just as you insure the contents of your house against various risks it is vital to do the same with your business. Loss from fire or theft, or accidental damage to equipment can cause serious financial embarrassment. Ensure you are adequately covered for the maximum value of contents and stock in trade.

PUBLIC LIABILITY INSURANCE

Public liability policies cover you in respect of your legal liability to pay damages related to bodily injury of any person and loss of or damage to property caused by accidents associated with your business. This cover relates to third parties, not your employees or yourself. Rates vary according to the nature of the business of the property and the level of indemnity required.

EMPLOYERS' LIABILITY

As an employer and business owner you are obliged by law to have cover under the Employers' Liability (Compulsory Insurance) Act 1969, and subsequent amendments. The Act requires employers to take out and maintain approved insurance policies with appropriate insurers against liability for bodily injury or disease sustained by employees in the course of employment. Failure to do so can lead to a fine not exceeding £200. The certificate of insurance or an appropriate copy must be displayed at the place of work. There are some exemptions within the Act. If, for example, your employees are all related to you then you are exempt.

SPECIAL INSURANCE PACKAGES

Some insurance companies have put together packages of cover for specific types of trade and business. For example, you can get a shopkeeper's package which covers most risks to both buildings and contents associated with keeping a shop. Premiums are calculated on the type of business (the lowest include booksellers and florists and the highest, off-licences and tobacconists) and on the area in which the business is located. Premiums for tobacconists in Liverpool and Glasgow are four times those for florists in Leeds.

Key points

- Consider the possibility of a licence rather than a lease.

82

- Examine leases and licences very carefully. Do not hesitate to get professional advice, particularly if you are making a substantial or long-term commitment.

- Negotiate terms suited to your needs. Do not simply accept what is offered if it is not what you want.

- Only sign when you are sure the document meets your needs and after other regulations (such as town planning and building regulations) have been checked to ensure that your business can trade there.

- Make sure you comply with any conditions specified in the lease and deeds.

- Check your insurance liabilities. Tenants should clarify who is responsible for property cover.

- Decide what type and level of insurance you want.

Chapter 9

Managing the Move

The removal process

In considering the physical movement of stock, equipment and machinery you may be tempted to 'do it yourself'. For many very small businesses this will be a perfectly sensible economy. However, think back to the last time you moved house and remember all the difficulties and hard work involved. Remember too that there is little to be gained from using your own specialist employees as packers and porters when they should be doing their own jobs. You may be well advised to use professional removers who will have all the appropriate equipment. Always obtain at least three quotations as rates can vary significantly between companies. The major removal companies have special packages for industrial and commercial moves and if the movement of personnel is included a still more competitive deal may be given. Explain the details of the move and discuss all the various elements with the removal company representative. If old machinery or equipment is no longer needed, this can be stored or disposed of.

The success of a move depends to a large extent on thorough pre-planning. Most major removal companies will give you advice and leaflets which will help you plan the necessary arrangements. The key points to consider are:

- Give careful consideration to the layout of machinery, stock and furniture at your new location. Draw up a diagram of how you want things organised.
- Label all items with their new location: use different colours for each room or floor.
- Empty machines such as photocopiers of their processing fluid.
- Ensure that you have a handyman or electrician available at the new site to refit servicing systems or rewire electrical fittings.
- Take out appropriate additional insurance cover. Accidents can happen even with the best removal companies.

- Move only what you will need. Take the opportunity to weed out dead files and to ditch obsolete equipment or furniture.

On a more general level, in preparing for and managing the move, it is a good idea to start planning early. Relocation is a complex exercise and you should not under-estimate the time it will take to get things organised. Try to arrange the move for a slack period of the year. If possible this should be your normal holiday period or one of the long public holiday weekends. There may be advantages in planning the move so that both units are running simultaneously during a brief transition stage.

Given the overriding importance of maintaining trading levels, production and output, ensure that all the necessary stock, materials and ancillary services will be ready and available at the new site. Remember that new machinery often takes time to commission and any new employees will need a training and 'settling in' period. If possible, appoint one person to co-ordinate and control the entire movement operation and release him from as many other responsibilities as you can. Be sure to draw up a simple planning schedule covering the major aspects of the move (see the simplified illustration on page 84). Mark the dates at which various actions need to be taken, and check that the target dates are achieved. Some of the actions to be included are:

- Inform gas, water and electricity boards of your intentions.
- Arrange with British Telecom for the transfer of your telephone number if the move is local or for the re-direction of calls if a longer distance move necessitates a new number.
- Inform the Post Office of your change of address and arrange for the redirection of mail.
- Obtain quotations from removal companies.
- Inform suppliers and customers of the impending move and of your new address and telephone number.
- Arrange for headed paper and business cards to be produced with the new address and telephone number.

Moving employees

One of the major worries facing businesses which move long

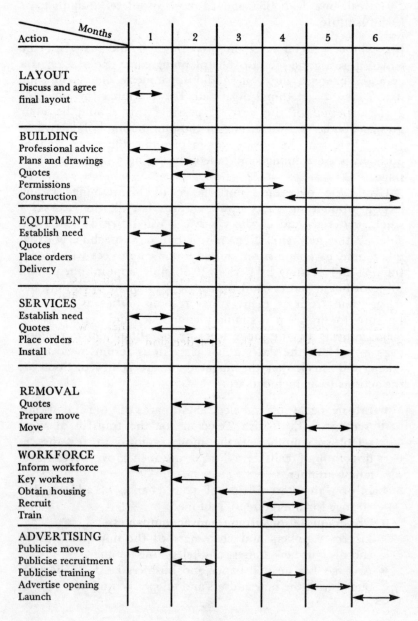

Moving premises: a simple planning schedule

distances is the loss of key personnel. The importance of this issue will depend on the number of highly qualified staff and the prospects of obtaining suitable replacements should this prove necessary. While the move will have positive benefits for the firm and its owner, quite frequently the workforce will see it as both uninvited and unwelcome. In general we are not a very mobile nation and moving from one community to another does not come easily. Usually it is the younger employees who are most willing to move. Do not rely on taking all your workforce with you. If the loss of employees is likely to be seriously disruptive, think again about relocation or make provisions to recruit and train staff at the new location well in advance of the move. You may also have to consider a redundancy policy.

Experience shows that there are several ways by which you may encourage the workforce to move with you:

INVOLVEMENT IN THE SEARCH FOR A NEW SITE
Inform the workforce at an early stage of your intention to move. Tell them exactly why the move is needed and what courses of action you are considering. If you have your own broad ideas about locations, ask them to indicate which they would prefer. Although the final decision will be yours, your workforce should be involved in the choice.

OFFER AN ASSISTANCE PACKAGE
Moving house and getting established in a new area is a major undertaking, fraught with risks and costs. Even the smallest company should put together a package deal for its employees to cover removal expenses and the search for a new house. The major removal companies will be able to help. The movement of staff and workers is often included within the overall removal package. You might also consider paying other expenses associated with moving, such as solicitors' and estate agents' fees, hotel accommodation for husband and wife while looking for a new house, and a disturbance allowance.

OFFER A FINANCIAL PACKAGE
You should not expect your workers to move without some reward. Many firms offer bonuses or increased salaries or wages for those who accompany the firm. A long distance move may also be an ideal opportunity to promote key personnel.

SELL THE AREA INTO WHICH YOU ARE MOVING

The new area may be unfamiliar to many of the workforce. A process of both familiarisation and hard sell will probably be necessary. You could use the skills of the local authority industrial development officials in this exercise. They will have brochures and promotional films of their area and what it has to offer. They will be able to help you explain the advantages of the area as a place to live. Key questions for most families revolve around houses and schools. The former may be a major attraction to the workforce if you are moving from the South East or other major industrial areas to an area of lower house prices.

Many companies take their workforce on an initial trip to familiarise them with the area. A day spent looking around, visiting the shopping centre and browsing through estate agents' information sheets can be a valuable exercise. It can of course go wrong. One London company took its entire workforce of 42 by coach to South Wales for the day to introduce the area and the new site. It rained all day so that what could be seen through the misted coach windows was viewed very unfavourably. On the way home the coach broke down and the party was delayed for three hours. Only two people moved with the firm.

TAKE ADVANTAGE OF ANY ASSISTANCE FOR TRANSFER OF WORKERS THAT YOUR NEW AREA MAY OFFER

Assistance does vary considerably from place to place. Many local authorities will try to help with council housing. Some offer a key worker scheme. In Northern Ireland, for example, where workers are transferred to fill new key posts, the package includes:

- Fares for the worker and spouse for preliminary visits and for the journey to take up employment.
- Weekly contribution towards temporary lodgings.
- Household removal expenses.
- Legal and other fees associated with buying and selling a house.

Publicising your move

Whatever the reason for your relocation, it is vital that it is properly advertised and receives good publicity. This publicity campaign should begin several weeks before your move and

continue for several weeks afterwards. It is important to publicise the move at both the old site and the new one. Inform
all your suppliers and customers of your change of address.
Produce a leaflet which includes a map of your new location.
Ensure that the agent dealing with your former property
indicates on the sale board that you have moved and not gone
out of business. Because of the recession a 'to let' sign frequently
indicates a company which has ceased trading. Place notices
on conspicuous parts of the building indicating where you are
moving to. In the case of local moves, for example a shop
moving from one part of the town centre to another, it is
useful to put up a simple map showing how to get to your
new address. Again in the case of shops, an opening sale with
special bargains may help to advertise your new location.

Persuade your major suppliers and companies which have
been involved with the development of the new site to place a
joint advert in the local press. You will have seen examples
where a complete page or even pages of a local paper are taken
over with an advertising feature about a new company. If
several parties are involved this can be a very economical way
of announcing your arrival. It may be appropriate to have an
'official opening' or 'press launch' as described in Chapter 11.

Keeping contacts

For many firms moving long distances, the danger of losing
contact with suppliers and customers is a major worry. This
concern, however, can be overstated. If you look at the geography of your business links you will probably find they
already cover a wide area. Although it is often suggested that
small businesses trade over a small area this is in fact rarely the
case. If you analyse the amount of face-to-face contact involved
in running your business (compared with telephone, telex and
other forms of communication) you will have an assessment of
the danger of dislocation. As many of your contacts will already
be outside the 'local' band of telephone charges, even these
costs will probably be little affected.

Companies who have moved longer distances usually suggest
that they have few, if any, problems in keeping their business
links. Indeed, many continue to trade with their former suppliers and customers as if no move had taken place. The obvious
exceptions are, of course, shops and professional services with a
local or neighbourhood clientele: in effect when such firms as

these move long distances they are not so much transferring operations as closing one business and opening another.

A move of any distance will take you into a new business environment which will offer you new opportunities. If you have moved to take advantage of a regional market you will already have given this serious thought. If not, this may be the time to think of new suppliers and customers. A firm new to an area will always be seen as an opportunity for the local business community who may be anxious to trade with you and even offer exceptionally competitive rates to attract your future custom. Do look around and use local directories to find services. Join the local Business Club and Chamber of Commerce or Trade; their newsletters can be a useful way of becoming known and meeting other local businessmen.

Key points

- If possible have one person in charge of planning the move.

- Try to move at a quiet time of the year.

- Prepare a timetable covering all the steps which need to be taken.

- Establish a personnel policy including selling the area to your staff, relocation assistance, salaries and promotion, new recruitment and redundancy. Check if the local authority offers a key worker assistance scheme.

- Take the measures necessary to ensure continuity of trading and production (for example, ordering of stock or materials).

- Discuss your move with customers and suppliers and inform them of your change of address and the date of the move.

- It is usually advisable to employ professional removers.

- Market and publicise your arrival in the new area.

- Take advantage of any fresh opportunities available in the new location: forge new contacts.

Chapter 10

Organising Your Property: Services, Layout and Environment

Introduction

When moving to different premises, whether newly built, second-hand or converted, you will need to consider their fitting out, layout and use. Ideally, you will have given some thought to these matters before selecting the premises. It is obviously preferable if the planning and preparatory work can be accomplished before moving in.

However, amid all the pressures on small business managers, compounded by relocation, it is tempting to regard detailed questions of space usage and interior design as merely frills; but it is unwise to dismiss these environmental considerations as secondary. Well thought out layouts and surroundings can actually contribute to the effective operation of your business and hence to its profitability. Insufficient attention to good space usage can result in a whole range of inefficiencies, delays, frustrations and even risks to health and safety. Poor conditions can erode your morale and that of your employees. It can also present a depressing and disorganised image to visitors and clients. Careful physical planning can avoid many of the psychological and functional difficulties which people often face at work.

Any move or extension should be used as an opportunity to reconsider and improve the layout and spatial arrangement of your work patterns and to develop more efficient modes of operation. Indeed, the stimulus of new premises should act as a catalyst for new ideas across all facets of the business.

In deciding precisely how much time, effort and money to expend on fitting out and decor you should first take account of your security of tenure. Obviously it makes sense to do more to a building which you own or which you hold on a long lease. The longer you intend to stay, the more benefits you will reap from any investment made. The more staff you employ and the larger the number of visiting clients, the stronger is the case for expenditure on environmental quality. Some premises will clearly require more attention than others, and some trades (such as fashion boutiques) are obviously more affected than others by questions of design, decor and image.

Certain measures will, however, be required by law. In preparing and using your premises you will need to comply with the safety regulations already referred to in Chapter 7. For example, you will need to satisfy the requirements of the local fire authorities. This may involve merely the purchase of some portable fire extinguishers or it could demand the installation of a sophisticated sprinkler system.

The range of work to be undertaken in getting premises ready for safe, efficient and comfortable use is extremely varied. This chapter classifies these tasks into two main groups: the provision of basic environmental services (such as heating and lighting) and the question of layout, design and decor. Separate sections look in more detail at the special requirements of shops and offices.

Basic services

If you are moving to established premises previously used for a business similar to your own, basic services should already be provided. However, if you are moving into brand-new premises, the developer may well have adopted a 'bare shell' approach leaving you to do part of the fitting out. In recent years the degree of completion achieved by developers has fallen. This reduces their costs and avoids the danger of providing finishes or fittings which might not actually be suited to the tenant's particular requirements. Even so, the developer's 'bare shell' will normally include mains services (electricity, gas where available, and water), toilets and washing facilities.

ELECTRICITY SERVICES
The supply in Great Britain is normally single phase, 240 volts at 60Hz. If you are a manufacturer and need to install a three-phase supply this can be obtained by contacting the local electricity board. There are no standard charges; quotations will be given for each individual application.

In new units the internal electric wiring and the provision of sockets is often left to the tenant in order to allow maximum discretion in the use of space. A clear view of your intended operational layout is therefore essential before deciding on the distribution system and the number and location of sockets.

In old premises some adjustments to the system may be needed to meet your needs. A property survey undertaken prior to occupation will indicate whether general rewiring is needed.

HEATING

In planning heating arrangements you will need to take account of the building's geographical orientation, its insulation qualities, the level of comfort required and the costs of installation and operation. In practice, electric units (night-storage radiators, fan heaters and radiant heaters) are the most common method of heating small business premises, principally because the installation costs are relatively low. Night-storage radiators have the benefit of off-peak tariffs and with their new slim lines occupy less space than previously. Fan and radiant heaters are more immediately responsive to sudden drops in temperature and can be more easily moved if layouts have to be changed.

Adequate ventilation not only can assist in the control of temperature but also is essential for a healthy working environment with sufficient oxygen and minimum smells and fumes. Doors and windows may provide enough ventilation. In addition a variety of power-driven ventilation fans are available which control the inward and/or outward movement of air.

LIGHTING

Lighting methods should reflect both the installation costs and the day-to-day running charges. Artificial lighting can be used not only to compensate for inadequate daylight but also as an attractive feature of interior design. When fluorescent tubes are used you should ensure that the diffusers are cleaned regularly and that you have a ready supply of spare tubes and spotlight bulbs.

TELEPHONES

Your choice of telephone system will be influenced by the size and nature of your business and by the level of communication you need within the premises. Systems are available which will provide an external line with extensions which can make both external calls and calls to other extensions within the building. Alternatively you may prefer a completely independent internal network. If you have a number of relatively unsupervised staff your arrangements should take account of the danger of unauthorised personal calls. When fitting out a new building the telephone system ought to be planned sufficiently early to avoid unnecessary damage to decoration and carpets at the time of installation.

SECURITY

How much to spend on the security of your premises and on intruder prevention will depend on the value of the goods held in stock and the degree of disruption which burglary or vandalism could impose. Having your premises broken into can give rise to a lot of extra work. You may, for example, have to deal not only with the police but with the insurance company, disappointed clients, a building repairer and with suppliers whose help is needed for emergency re-stocking. It is wise to take good precautions. Indeed your insurance company is likely to insist on it.

Burglary prevention can be achieved by physical barriers and/or alarms. The barriers can take the form of metal grilles or burglar bars over windows, thick security window glazing, collapsible metal gates in entrances and the use of sophisticated mortise locks. Alarms generally use a continuous electric current flowing in a closed circuit which, if broken, causes the alarm to sound. There are many different kinds of alarm available on the market, each with particular specifications and advantages.

Careful internal layout can be a great help in security matters. A reception desk, customer service or purchase point placed so that the movement of people in and out of premises can be monitored may save you losses from theft. You can obtain expert guidance on property security from the crime prevention officers of your local police force. If asked they will visit your property, identify areas of vulnerability and suggest the kinds of measures which ought to be taken.

Layout and decor

ORGANISING SPACE

Moving to a different property presents an opportunity to re-examine your business activities and review how the various operations should be organised. Consideration of new layouts and redecoration, however, should not be limited to businesses moving location. All firms could benefit from this review process (without the associated cost of moving) if they simply took time to consider this area of their activities. Obviously the larger the business and premises, the greater the scope for alternative layouts. For the very smallest business some of the discussion below may seem less relevant but it is worth bearing in mind that the smaller the space the greater the need for its effective use.

In thinking about layouts it is helpful to begin by identifying the various stages or sections within the firm's operations and to ask:

- How much space does each activity require?
- Is the process or activity relatively footloose within the property or does it have particular locational needs?
- Does it have special requirements for access to other parts of the business?
- What are its major lines of communication which need to be accommodated or encouraged?

By addressing these issues you can build up a picture of the spatial arrangement of your firm's various activities and the movement requirements for materials, stock and employees. For example, you may identify incompatible activities such as those requiring concentration or creativity and those generating noise and disturbance. These two groups should be separated if possible, whereas mutually supportive or complementary functions should be brought together. In small workshops the installation of a simple mezzanine (an area of raised floor space) can create additional space while also allowing some segregation of activities. A desk and filing cabinet on the mezzanine will provide excellent office space and the void beneath can be used for storage.

The human factor is important too. By careful design and use of space it may be possible to reduce the potential for conflict between opposing personalities. Indeed, before committing yourself to a particular layout you should, formally or informally, discuss the alternatives with your employees. They may have some useful ideas and in any event could justifiably feel that they ought to be consulted. The planning process may also benefit from the use of physical models or at least scale diagrams showing spaces, machinery, fittings, furnishings and lines of communication. Paper 'cut-outs' of each movable item will help you to test a variety of layouts. Computer enthusiasts might even use graphics software to help visualise alternative designs from different perspectives.

All this may sound rather ambitious and it must be admitted that the scope for alternative layouts will depend on the building. An open-plan unit will offer *carte blanche* whereas the same area already divided into rooms and corridors represents a very different problem. Without major conversion work, the present physical structure will inevitably impose constraints on what can be achieved in the future. To be realistic, the planning process must therefore work from both ends and ask not only, 'What kind of space does this activity need?' but also, 'Given the environment we have, how can it best be used?' The perfect layout for your business will almost certainly not be practicable in the building you have, but by envisaging an ideal layout you will become better aware of your property's limitations. Although these limitations are to some extent inescapable, they can be moderated by changes in the way you operate. You may, for example, initiate regular visits and checks on staff working in areas remote from your own centre of operations. You must recognise the problems which your building creates and then seek to minimise them by adjusting your work and behaviour paterns.

DIRECTORS' OR OWNER MANAGERS' OFFICES

The space which may be of most concern are the directors' offices. They will want an environment appropriate to their status but not so extravagant as to disgruntle staff working in inferior conditions. Given the stresses of small business management, directors may be tempted to design a sanctuary where they can obtain some respite and peace of mind. Certainly, there will be times when a quiet place is essential to allow special concentration or confidential discussions. However, also bear in mind that if directors isolate themselves too far from other areas of operation, they may get out of touch and find it difficult to supervise employees.

RECEPTION AREAS

Another place of particular significance is the reception area. First impressions count and if large numbers of clients will be calling at the site you need to provide an attractive waiting area with appropriate seating, tables and magazine racks. The client must be made to feel welcome and comfortable. The reception area provides an ideal opportunity to show off your products and services and to advertise your professional qualifications and experience. Display cases are a good way of demonstrating both the variety and quality of your work. They must, however, be kept up to date, as neglected displays can easily become eye-sores and create a negative impression.

ADVERTISING

In order that clients and other visitors can identify your premises, one or more signs should be displayed on the outside of the building. These should be placed in a prominent position where they will attract the most attention. In addition to naming the firm it is usual to identify the trade and include the firm's logo if it has one. The lettering can be illuminated, painted by sign-writers or cut out from plastic, metal or wood. Illuminated signs are obviously visible at the greatest distance. The style of the lettering (modern, traditional etc) can be used to convey the firm's image. Lower-case letters use about 15 per cent less space than capitals and may be essential where space is limited.

Signs and advertisements attached to buildings are subject to town planning controls. The regulations are complex and in the white paper 'Lifting the Burden' the government has announced its intention of introducing a simpler system. At present, however, the position in broad outline is that planning consent is needed for signs and advertisements if any of the following conditons apply:

- If they are illuminated.
- If they include letters more than 0.75m high.
- If they are above 4.6m from the ground.
- If they are above the bottom level of the first-floor windows.
- If they are on a shop wall without a display window.

Still tighter controls are enforced in 'Areas of Special Control' (mainly sensitive rural locations). In addition, all directional signs on or near a public highway require the approval of the local highway authority (normally the county council) or the Department of Transport. The basic rationale behind all these controls is the protection of public safety and the visual appeal of the landscape.

DECORATION

In seeking to improve the visual appearance of your own premises (particularly if they are old and dilapidated), a new coat of paint can go a long way. When money is tight, it helps if you are prepared to do your own painting and decorating and certainly if you are taking on old premises an aptitude for DIY can be a major advantage. In choosing interior colours do take account of their psychological effects and the atmosphere they create; blues seem cool and quiet, reds are hot and

97

loud, greens and yellows are fresh and restful. Dark tones can be depressing, light tones are more cheerful. The careful use of colour can also change a room's perceived proportions. A small room may benefit from a light tone to encourage an illusion of space. A ceiling which is too high can be 'lowered' by dark shades. Tastes in colour are very personal and unless you intend to adopt a unified colour system throughout the property, staff with their own offices or work spaces could be allowed to make their own selections.

FURNISHINGS
In choosing furnishings it is important to take account of the psychological dimension. An oval table is less forbidding than a rectangular one and reduces the risk of people being apparently grouped into opposing camps. Furniture with futuristic designs or in modern materials, such as plastic or chrome, creates an avant-garde impression which may be right for a 'hi-tech' firm but inappropriate for a solicitor. On a more cosmetic note, a few indoor plants can help humanise an otherwise austere setting.

INTERIOR DESIGN
Ideally, interior design should be undertaken by a trained professional. If environment and image are really crucial it may well be worth hiring an interior designer. The professional will not only offer guidance on furniture, fabrics, colour and lighting, but will bring them together to achieve a harmonious total effect. If you are unsure about what the approximate costs might be of what you have in mind, a preliminary approach to one or two local interior designers (perhaps from Yellow Pages) can be useful. If the likely costs sound high, remember that professional help can avoid your making expensive mistakes and can also save you a lot of trouble by taking responsibility for actually getting the work done. Through their knowledge of local craftsmen and suppliers, designers can also ensure high levels of workmanship. Remember that designers are accustomed to working within tight budgets, and 'making a little go a long way' is one of the skills of the trade. You could therefore specify a sum and see what you could get for your money.

It helps if you can select your designer through personal recommendation. Better still write to the Designer Selection Service, The Design Council, 28 Haymarket, London SW1Y

4SU. Send in a brief outline of the kind of work to be done and they will suggest a small number of local firms. Many architects also undertake interior design work. Lists of local architects can be obtained from the Clients Advisory Service, Royal Institute of British Architects, 66 Portland Square, London W1N 4AD.

Having built up a shortlist, a phone call to each will determine whether he or she would be interested in your particular project and if so, you can then arrange a meeting. Ask for the names of firms for whom the designer has done similar work previously so that you can contact references and go and see examples of that work. Personal taste varies so much in matters of decor that it is important to find a designer whose style you like. In making the final selection do bear in mind that the cheapest fee or quote may not necessarily be the best value for money. Further information on selecting a designer, alternative methods of charging and on the various stages in the design process, is available in *How to Work with an Interior Designer* by William Turner, published by the Architectural Press (1981).

MAINTENANCE AND MONITORING
The issues of design, layout and environment addressed in this chapter are not 'once and for all' questions and it is important to note the need for continuing maintenance and review. Decor, lighting and furnishings will all need to be maintained and cleaned to prolong their life-span and protect their appearance. This is not to recommend an obsessive concern for a pristine environment. A degree of creative clutter should be accepted as a desirable and inevitable fact of business life. However, it is essential at the very least to undertake regular cleaning and to budget for redecoration and the replacement of carpets, furniture and fittings.

Finally, from time to time you will need to review and re-think your environment in the light of experience. Pre-planned layouts and spatial arrangements rarely work out exactly as forecast and may require subsequent adjustment. The environment will also need to adapt to changes in the scale and nature of your business. For example, if you move up-market, your decor may need to respond accordingly. Constant reorganisation is not to be recommended as repeated disruption to staff and customers can damage your business. However, occasional changes in layout can have a refreshing effect. Invention, imagination and new ideas can begin to flow after reorganisation.

Shops

A distinctive feature of the retail environment is the need to accommodate goods and, above all, encourage their purchase. At shop premises it is important, therefore, not only to maximise the sales space but also to make it convenient and attractive for customers. Space for auxiliary functions such as storage and office work is by comparison of secondary importance.

Although different shops have different needs there are a number of general guidelines for the layout of sales areas.

1. Perimeter walls are normally used for display fittings or counters, with the main floor area subdivided into display islands, known as gondolas, which should run lengthwise from front to rear forming a series of circulation corridors. Cul-de-sacs or dead-ends should generally be avoided. Shopfitters' charges vary substantially but grocery store gondolas, supplied and installed, might cost about £120 per metre or £150 per metre for double-sided gondolas.
2. Commodities should be arranged spatially so that similar or related products are grouped together. This is convenient for customers and helps them develop an accurate 'mental map' of the shop's layout. Incompatible products (for example canned meat and pet foods) should be kept well apart.
3. Some high demand goods should be placed at the rear of the shop so that customers have to pass a wide variety of other goods. This promotes impulse buying of goods noticed in passing.
4. The layout should allow easy supervision and minimise the threat of shoplifting. Entrances and exits should be easily monitored. Fixtures should not exceed about 4ft 6in in height. Small and costly items should be placed near the check-out to facilitate their security. Spaces behind columns are particularly at risk and should not be used for value commodities. Unavoidable blind spots can be covered by anti-theft mirrors or by closed-circuit television.
5. Special attention should be given to the shop entrance and above all to the window display since this plays a key role in enticing customers into the shop. Windows should be well-lit, colourful and eye-catching. They should display the full range and variety of products available inside. Specially promoted lines should be in a prominent position.

The display should be changed regularly both to avoid merchandise deterioration and to engage the passer-by's interest. In recent years some grocery shops and super-markets have abandoned traditional window displays and instead use the windows as poster space to advertise special offers. In this case it is important to keep the posters looking clean, colourful and up to date.

Further information on shop layouts and environments is provided in *Running Your Own Shop* by Roger Cox, published by Kogan Page (1985). Another useful text is *Shops: a manual of planning and design* by David Mun, published by the Architectural Press (1981).

Offices

In designing office environments an issue which has attracted particular interest and debate has been the merits of open-plan layouts. This is a subject too complex for exhaustive treatment here, and in any event, for those very small businesses operating in conventional rooms the idea of open-plan may be impractical. Therefore, the key arguments are presented here only in summary form.

The main benefits of open-plan are:

- It reduces building and fitting out costs by reducing the number of walls and doors and by allowing larger continuous floor coverings and light fittings.
- It promotes communication and team work. Individuals develop an enhanced awareness of their contribution to the enterprise as a whole.
- It encourages a spread of the work load between neighbours.
- It facilitates supervision and monitoring of employees' work and behaviour.
- It provides large, uninterrupted floor areas with maximum flexibility in the spatial arrangement of functions and staff.

However, the excessive optimism of the pioneers of open-plan has, in the light of experience, given way to a rather more sceptical view. The key objections to it are:

- It can be as agoraphobic as the traditional box-like offices were claustrophobic. People need and enjoy a degree of privacy and territoriality. Being exposed to public

101

surveillance all day can be psychologically wearing.

- Open-plan erodes the peace and solitude which can be essential for creativity, confidential discussions and for work requiring sustained concentration. The hubbub and mêlée of the office, the ringing of telephones and the chatter of colleagues can be distracting and irritating and may lower the general level of performance.
- Senior staff may feel that their status demands a separate office.

At the heart of the open-plan debate lies the conflict between the need for collective co-operation and individual privacy. One way of attempting to resolve this dilemma is to use a system of movable partitions. Together with good carpeting these can provide useful sound-proofing as well as a degree of visual screening and privacy. The partitions can be high enough to be exclusive, but low enough for people to look over, or a combination of both according to individual needs and circumstances. These mobile walls have the benefit of considerable flexibility and can also be used for attaching information boards, displays, racks and shelves.

Given the confined conditions in which many small businesses operate it is common practice for two or more people to share the same office space, either in a proper room or a partitioned enclave. This raises the question of how to arrange desks in a shared environment. If employees sit at desks facing each other the result is often not only a loss of privacy but also a surfeit of unproductive conversation. However, sitting one behind the other seems too overtly unfriendly, and the one being watched from the rear will feel uncomfortable and ill-at-ease. Sitting side by side is therefore generally to be preferred. An alternative is for staff to face each other but at an angle rather than directly in line. This avoids both the 'eye-balling' problem and the feeling of surveillance from behind. In this question of desk arrangement, as in other layout matters, you will in practice be guided both by the preferences of the particular individuals involved and by the size and configuration of the space available.

Key points

- The opportunity to rethink the layout of your work patterns and, if possible, to improve working conditions is always available. You do not have to wait until you move.

- Consider how much time, effort and money to devote to the physical environment (you must at least satisfy the minimum statutory requirements). Remember that good surroundings are more than an aesthetic frill.

- Ensure an appropriate electricity supply, wiring network and socket distribution (preferably before decorating).

- Consider the heating, lighting, ventilation, telephone and security arrangements.

- On matters of layout and decor consult your staff.

- Identify the various functions within your business and determine their preferred spatial arrangement: be prepared for compromises.

- Experiment (on paper at least) with different layouts for equipment and furniture.

- Recognise and respond to the danger that the building may foster undesirable work/behaviour patterns.

- How important is an attractive reception area?

- Put up appropriate name signs and advertisements. Check the planning regulations.

- Consider the need for internal redecoration and new furnishings. Might professional design help be worthwhile?

- Do not neglect maintenance and repair.

- Both layout and decor should be reviewed and if necessary up-dated from time to time.

- Retailers should give priority to the sales space and to an attractive customer environment. Think about circulation flows, the arrangement of different commodities and how to minimise shoplifting and maximise impulse buying.

- Offices. Review, if relevant, the 'pros' and 'cons' of open-plan. Are movable partitions right for you? Remember the psychology of desk arrangements.

Chapter 11

Property Conversion and Subdivision

Introduction

Conversion and subdivision are two methods of obtaining premises often overlooked by small businesses. If you cannot find the type of premises you want, conversion of an existing building can provide 'tailor-made' premises to meet your exact requirements. If you need less space than you currently possess and are thinking of moving to smaller premises, subdivision can avoid the problems and costs of relocation. By leasing out your spare space you can obtain an additional income and provide a useful means of diversifying your firm's activities. For the business willing to turn its hand to small-scale property devleopment both conversion and subdivision can bring quick economic returns. As the two case studies in Chapter 12 describing conversion and subdivision show, money can be recouped very quickly. A recent study by two of the authors found that the costs of conversion and subdivision were often covered by the first year's rental income.

The activities involved in converting and subdividing premises are broadly similar. Both usually require the construction of extra walls and doorways, some liaison with local authority planning and building officials, and the marketing and management of the premises. You may be interested in a conversion scheme either to accommodate your own business or to produce premises to sell or lease on to another firm. Conversion can be possible in a wide range of buildings. It is not always necessary for the premises to have been used as business accommodation. Residential houses, old tram depots, schools, churches and even mortuaries have all been converted into various types of small business premises.

In the present economic situation, although the market for small premises has remained relatively buoyant, medium- and larger-scale properties have found fewer buyers. This has led to a fall in prices and has created the opportunity to purchase cheap larger properties and convert them into the smaller units which are more in demand. Some small businesses unable to find suitable premises have taken advantage of this situation. They have bought larger premises than they needed at relatively cheap prices (per square foot), converted whatever amount they needed for themselves and then leased or sold the remainder (as one or more small business units) to other firms. In this way they have obtained premises tailor-made to their own needs and made a profit out of the remainder of the building.

The process of subdividing premises and renting out spare space can take many forms. It may involve simply separating off an unused area by a chalk line on the floor. More substantial schemes involve the construction of walls, doorways, toilets and washing facilities. It might be thought that subdivision is only useful for declining firms no longer making full use of their premises. This is not necessarily the case. Even expanding firms often find that technological innovation and the introduction of new plant and machinery allow increased production from a reduced floor area.

Next time you are at work look at the space around you and assess whether it is fully used. Is any spare capacity needed for business expansion (an entirely legitimate use of space) or is it simply surplus to requirements? A tidying up and reorganization of your premises and the removal of redundant machinery or furniture might give you the extra space needed for a subdivision scheme. If you are unsure about the benefits of subdivision, calculate how much in rates, insurance, maintenance, heating, lighting and either rent or interest repayments your underused space is costing. You might well be surprised.

Because many leases (particularly those covering periods of less than five years) do not permit substantial internal reorganisation or subletting, it is usually necessary to own premises before you can consider undertaking conversion or subdivision. But some landlords have agreed to rewrite leases and allow tenants to create smaller units. The main advantage for landlords is that their premises are converted, at no cost to them, into the size of units currently in demand by the market.

Most small firms regard a move into property management as a quantum leap in business practice. A fear of the unknown and concern about high costs are common reasons for a lack of action. The remainder of this chapter will therefore seek to provide basic information on how to manage conversion and subdivision efficiently. Certainly worries about costs need not be justified. By avoiding expensive construction work and doing some jobs in-house, costs can be kept to a minimum and may often be recovered within the first year or two of operation. Moreover, as explained in Chapter 6, government grants and tax relief may be available to offset relocation and property development costs.

Market research

Some degree of market research is normally essential for developments which will produce units to sell or rent out. It is obviously important to identify what kinds of premises are in demand and how much return you can expect to make from your investment. The scale of the research will depend on how many units you are producing and the size of your investment. If you simply intend to let out a spare room or disused workshop, with minimal building expenditure, then your 'research' will be limited to a brief assessment of the prospects for success. Similarly, market research is of little immediate importance where conversions are being undertaken solely for your own use although you will want to take into account the possible resale value of your premises in the future. Where market research really counts is with larger-scale projects providing several small units. In such cases detailed research is essential to direct your investment in the most profitable way and, if necessary, to persuade financial organisations to provide the money. You will need to understand small firms' property requirements and to determine the level of demand for the kind of accommodation you have in mind. Many of these issues have been described in previous chapters.

You will need information on the following items:

- *Rent levels in the local market.* An assessment of rental levels per square foot will indicate how much to spend on building work. This issue will be essential in budgeting to ensure a good return on your investment.
- *Size of premises.* The sizes of units most in demand should be identified. In multi-unit developments, construction work should ideally allow for later flexibility in the unit sizes. This will permit existing businesses to expand *in situ* (where possible) and will provide a range of units of different sizes to be available for prospective tenants. A miscalculation in your assessment of size should therefore not have irreversible consequences.

- *Likely users.* It is important to find out which types of business are most in need of premises. Industry, office, retail and storage oriented businesses will each have different requirements. They will also be willing to pay different levels of rent.
- *Location.* Locational needs will obviously vary with the kinds of business tenants you have in mind. Within your locality, which are the most attractive areas for your prospective tenants? How are locational preferences likely to change in future?
- *Facilities required.* The level of service provision will, in part, depend upon what rents can be achieved. Electricity and telephones are required by nearly all businesses. Other considerations are ground floor access, three-phase electricity, artificial ventilation, display/sales areas, gas, extra lighting and strengthened floors to take heavy equipment. If a development is to be intensively serviced, telex, typing, accounting, bookkeeping, computing and photocopying services could also be required. This type of intensively serviced accommodation is really at the very upper end of the market. The majority of conversion and subdivision schemes simply provide a bare shell with electricity to a junction box. The various extras outlined above are by no means necessary, although they can help to attract tenants.

SOURCES OF INFORMATION

The best sources of information and advice on your local property market are the different groups currently involved in it. Guidance should be sought from:

- *Estate agents.* They may tend to be over-optimistic about the potential benefits of new development. Try approaching them as if you were looking for premises as this could reveal a more accurate picture of the state of the market. Exploratory discussions with estate agents are free; they do not charge on a time basis as is the case, for example, with solicitors.
- *The local authority.* Many local authorities have in recent years built small units particularly for industry. Ask the estates department about the take-up of their property and about tenant turnover and rental levels. If the local authority has an economic or industrial development officer (and most now do) they too should have some

ideas on what types of premises are required by the groups approaching them for help. Many local authorities have concentrated on factories and industrial estate provision and will therefore be most expert in this field.

- *Enterprise agencies and business organisations.* Enterprise agencies offer advice to small businesses and are often approached by start-up firms or other businesses looking for premises. Chambers of Commerce and Trade, small business centres and clubs will all have views on the kinds of property most needed locally.
- *Local newspapers.* Look at both the 'property available' and 'property wanted' columns. There may be developers advertising premises similar to those you have in mind. Contact them to see if you can gauge the level of response they have had to their adverts (but be careful not to present yourself as a competitor in the market place). Firms advertising in the 'property wanted' columns can be contacted to ask for further details of what they are looking for.
- *A look around your locality.* Some small premises will only be advertised by billboards on the site. A tour of the area is essential, therefore, in gaining an impression of the state of the market.

Site evaluation and selection

If you are thinking of subdividing your existing premises then obviously you will not be faced with property searches and making comparative assessments of different sites. You will, however, still need to determine how suitable your existing property is for subdivision. If you are looking for new premises, use the search methods discussed in Chapter 4 and then make your choice. In either case do remember that some sites will lend themselves more readily to subdivision than others and that on complex technical matters you may need professional advice from a surveyor, architect or someone with experience in property development.

In making a site evaluation you should try to assess how closely the property would satisfy the patterns of demand uncovered by your market research. Is the location likely to prove attractive to your prospective client group? In addition you will also need to assess how easily and cheaply the subdivision work could be accomplished. For example, the size and shape of the building is important. Long narrow structures are more easily subdivided than large square spaces. Single-storey buildings are easier to develop as many of the problems associated with floor loadings, access and fire regulations do not arise. There are also advantages in sites which contain a number of separate buildings. If your own company occupies one of these, building work on the others can proceed without seriously disturbing your own business operations. This arrangement can also minimise security problems. Obviously you will need to check roofs, look for signs of damp and assess the building's general condition in the usual way. You should also check whether there are any town planning, building regulations or other legal restrictions which might cause difficulties (see Chapter 7). Remember that subdivision and the resulting increased level of use could place greater demands on access points, surrounding roads and car parking. These are all matters of interest to the local planning authority. Make sure, too, that the property deeds are checked to ensure that there are no restrictive covenants which would prohibit your proposals.

Design and construction

The type and size of unit(s) you develop will be guided by your market research. If the demand for large premises in your area is still relatively buoyant you may not need to carry out much subdivision and building work. If smaller units are preferable you will need to decide carefully how best to sub-divide the premises. It is usually advisable to make full use of existing entrances, services (including toilets), walls and partitions. When constructing new walls or partitions you will have to consider two features: flexibility and insulation. A flexible layout, allowing sizes of units to be varied, will usually be constructed of plaster board walls which offer poor noise and heat insulation. Well insulated units constructed of brick or breeze block walls are more expensive and offer much less flexibility. Think carefully about which type of wall or com-bination of both is best for your purposes.

In the most straightforward cases subdivision may only involve building a wall and a doorway. However, the larger and more complex the building programme, the more likely it is that you will need professional advice. One way of avoiding architects' fees is to persuade your local university or poly-technic architecture department to use your building as a student project. If you do hire professional architects make sure they do not 'over-design'. Most small firms do not expect the highest levels of environmental finish or decoration. However, poor conditions will deter potential tenants. Seek to provide a basic but wholesome environment, and if particular tenants need additional or superior facilities they can provide them to meet their own individual requirements.

In deciding how much you should spend on property purchase and building work and decoration, there is a general rule of thumb that costs should not exceed five or six times the annual rental. In the majority of cases costs will be far lower than this upper limit. However, do talk to your accountant and see what rate of return he recommends. One way of phasing your expenditure is to stage the work over several months. This gradual approach places fewer demands on company cash flow and allows you to learn from experience. More gloomily, it may also fit in with a planned reduction of your main business operations and the resulting phased release of space.

The actual construction work can be undertaken at varying degrees of cost, quality and speed. Small self-employed builders are relatively cheap but sometimes lack the manpower and resources to complete a job quickly. Jobbing and contract builders usually have better resources and complete work faster but can be more expensive. The cheapest option is to complete the work yourself with the help of your friends or workforce. An aptitude for DIY can be a great advantage in small-scale property development. Whatever your approach, do put safety first. Seek building regulations approval and check whether a new fire certificate will be needed.

Marketing

If the market research undertaken earlier has been carried out carefully there should be no serious problems in finding tenants for your new units, but it is still essential to develop a positive marketing strategy. You may need to use several different methods:

- *Bill boards.* Surprising as it may seem, one of the most successful ways of advertising vacant industrial or commercial property is the use of bill boards, particularly if the site is on a main road. At some developments this has been the only method used to attract tenants. Bill boards have the great advantage of being cheap.

- *Estate agents.* Whether using an estate agent is worth the cost will depend on the probability of your being able to obtain tenants by other, cheaper means. Agents' fees do vary, so shop around and check on precisely what you will get for your money. For example, will you have to pay extra for advertising? Typical agents' fees are 2 or 2½ per cent for freehold premises and about 10 per cent of the annual rent for leases. Some agents operate a scale of fees with lower rates for larger and more valuable properties. The cost may be reduced if you give an agent sole agency status. He may also work harder on selling your premises because he knows that he will get the fee. Do make clear, in writing, that you will only pay if he is instrumental in obtaining a tenant. With a sole agency arrangement it is wise at the outset to impose a time limit, perhaps three months, so that if a tenant has not been found you are free to try another agent. In choosing an estate agent be sure to select a reputable firm with a strong industrial and commercial department. It is often suggested that estate agents do not make much money out of small property transactions and are therefore not particularly energetic in selling them. Certainly an agent is likely to be more interested and more useful to you if you have a suite of small units to offer rather than a single small property.
- *Local newspapers.* Placing an advertisement in the local paper is cheap and the results are usually good. Be sure to place the advert on the newspaper's property day.
- *Property lists.* Your local authority estates, planning or economic development department may well produce lists of vacant business premises, though often these focus mainly on industrial properties. Inclusion is usually free. Local business organisations and enterprise agencies may perform a similar service.
- *A press launch.* If your development is on a sufficient scale, your marketing strategy could culminate in an official opening or press launch. This sounds rather grand but only involves providing some wine and a buffet lunch and need not be too expensive. As well as the media, invite local authority officials and representatives from local business organisations. Newspapers, free weeklies, radio and television are always on the look-out for local

111

events. If properly nurtured they could provide useful publicity for you, particularly if your scheme involves job creation, a building with a varied and interesting history, or other newsworthy material. Distribute handouts and promotional literature to all visitors.

Management

If your development involves a considerable number of units you may prefer to subcontract the management, tenant selection and rent-collecting functions to another specialist company or an estate agent. If, however, you wish your own firm to carry out these duties, it is best to designate one person as site manager and to notify your tenants accordingly. This simplifies lines of communication and prevents time-consuming approaches to other staff within your firm. The use of retired managers is another solution which has been used with success.

You will need to consider carefully the form and content of any lease which you offer tenants. Information on leases has already been given in Chapter 7 but remember this time to read it from the landlord's point of view!

The range of possible rent levels will be given by your market research. It is worth considering how you will present rents: rents inclusive or exclusive of rates and any service charges, rents per square foot or as a lump sum for a given space (see Chapter 4). The collection of rents should be done on site either weekly or monthly in advance. This is best undertaken by the site manager as it allows a regular point of contact between landlord and tenant and a useful link for the exchange of information. A bookkeeping system will be needed to record and monitor charges, as well as an auditing system for all financial transactions. Other management items which you will need to consider include the security of premises and their contents, insurance, maintenance, repair and the day-to-day caretaking arrangements, if any. Further information on evaluating and managing subdivision schemes is contained in *Putting Spare Space to Work* by Howard Green, Paul Foley and Irene Burford, published by the Small Business Research Trust, London (1985).

Key points

INTRODUCTORY APPRAISAL
- Do you have unused space? How much is it costing you?

- Could a simple reorganisation of your premises produce spare space?

MARKET RESEARCH
- What kinds of business are seeking accommodation?
- What is the level of demand?
- What kinds of units are most sought after?

SITE EVALUATION
- Are the premises in an appropriate location?
- Does the site layout lend itself to development?
- Is there sufficient room for circulation, access and parking?
- Are there any legal restrictions which could frustrate your plans?

DESIGN AND CONSTRUCTION
- Plan the layout, design and servicing arrangements.
- Obtain financial support if needed and grants if available.
- Do not neglect building and safety regulations.
- Construction: if only small-scale work is neeed can you use your own employees?

MARKETING
- Work out a marketing strategy.
- Be sure to use a bill board.
- Contact all the sources of free advertising.
- Consider using estate agents.
- Consider a press launch.

MANAGEMENT
- Decide on a management system.
- What type of lease will you use?
- What rents will you charge?
- Make sure the building is adequately insured.

Chapter 12

Case Studies

Introduction

The previous chapters have outlined and illustrated the range of industrial and commercial property issues relevant to the small businessman. In this final chapter, eight case studies are presented which show how individual businesses have approached the property issue in relation to their own development. While the case studies have been chosen because they illustrate specific problems which have been discussed earlier, they reveal the wider context within which decisions about property are taken. Readers may be able to identify with these problems in at least one of the case studies and gain a better understanding of issues relevant to their own business. The case studies have been divided into four groups to highlight particular property issues.

WORKING FROM HOME
Steve Hancock and Stewart Johnston, the owners of two very different businesses, illustrate the problems and benefits of working from home. The car repair business is typically unwelcome in residential areas: Steve Hancock's mobile service provided a very practical solution to this problem. Stewart Johnson, a part-time businessman, has already experienced many of the problems of working from home, although in both cases working from home has had the advantage of keeping costs and overheads to a minimum.

FIRST PREMISES
Cedars Hotel and Peppercorn Wholefoods emphasise the problems of starting a business and finding first premises. In both cases locational factors were of great importance. The Barley and Carter families, both involved with the Cedars Hotel, undertook a very systematic search for their first hotel. When obtaining their first property, Joan and Frank Savage, proprietors of Peppercorn Wholefoods, were confronted with less than scrupulous landlords and short-term lease agreements.

They soon realised the importance of location for the retail trade. Following a short move, they were able to learn from their experience and develop a very profitable health food shop.

MOVING PREMISES

General, Marine and Life, and Leyland Industrial Cases both experienced the problems associated with a change of location: General, Marine and Life epitomises the problems for small businesses as they moved from working at home into more formal accommodation. For Tim Ingram, the proprietor, working from home eventually proved incompatible with the wishes of his neighbours, forcing him to enter the uncharted waters of leases, landlords and subletting. Leyland Golley moved over 300 miles from Bolton to Cornwall, prompted by a variety of non-business reasons. Leyland also became a landlord, letting out space which he had acquired and which was surplus to his requirements.

CONVERSION AND SUBDIVISION

The final two case studies illustrate the advantages which can be gained by conversion and subdivision of property for industrial and commercial use. Both Allen Priest and Sons Ltd and Cox, Wilcox and Company illustrate the ease with which small businesses can diversify their activities and become small-scale property developers. For Cox, Wilcox and Company the subdivision of their property has allowed a planned reduction and eventual stabilisation of the existing metal manufacturing business. Allen Priest and Sons purchased premises considerably larger than their requirements. The rental income earned from their converted units has allowed them to develop their own business on a more secure basis.

Steve Hancock mobile car repair service

Steve Hancock began his car repair business in Ilkley, Yorkshire, in April 1982 having previously worked as a mechanic for a motor-cycle firm. He was concerned that his job was not very secure so he began to consider starting his own business. He already had experience of working on both cars and motor-cycles, which he thought he could put to better use.

As he lived in Ilkley it was important that the business was based there too. However, appropriate property in the Ilkley area for a small car repair service was not available at a price which Steve considered he could afford. Small units of various ages and types were available but rental levels were in the order of £45 per week. To travel to the nearby towns of Otley or Shipley for cheaper premises was inappropriate. In the end a mobile service appeared the obvious answer, using home as a base.

Most of his repair work is therefore done at other people's homes, or in the road outside, from a mobile workshop which Steve has equipped in a second-hand van. This has avoided many of the problems associated with home-based car repair businesses. The noise and nuisance is created at the client's address, but only at infrequent intervals. Steve readily admits that there are problems associated with his approach, perhaps the biggest being the weather, although he is now getting used to working in the wet and cold. To his clients he offers a very useful 'on the spot' service which avoids the difficulty of delivering the car to a garage. The van from which he works also acts as a ready advert for his work.

Although he spent some time planning the business before setting up on his own, Steve took little professional advice. It all seemed self-evident. He did, though, take many clients from his former employers. Although home is not the centre of the repair work, it is the office for the business and his wife answers the telephone and helps with the day-to-day administration. As they have four young children, there is usually someone in the house so an efficient reception service operates with minor domestic disturbance. Many of the other problems associated with working at home, such as constant domestic interruptions, are avoided because the actual work is undertaken away from home. Accounts and schedules are done in the quiet of the evening.

As he took no professional advice when he started up, Steve did not concern himself with town planning or any other possible limitations on using his home as a business base. Nor did he have any problems with neighbours about parking his rather large van outside the house. This was probably because in the semi-industrial area where be began the van did not intrude.

More recently the Hancocks have moved house, principally because with four children they needed more space. However, because of high property prices in Ilkley they were forced to move to Silsden, a small town some six or seven miles away. Property prices there allowed them to buy a larger house on a small estate. This estate environment had several effects on the business. First, while the large van had fitted in well at the previous house, Steve thought it appropriate to find a more suitable parking space, although he had received no direct complaints. He obtained rented space in a nearby builder's yard, and initially this was no problem, although it did add an additional journey to his schedule each day. However, because the van was no longer parked near a house, it was less secure, and as it contained valuable equipment it was a target for vandals. Eventually the parking space became unavailable so a new solution was needed. Second, the new house was some six or seven miles away from most of his clients, and increased petrol costs became a worry. Both these factors finally forced Steve into buying a different van, much smaller and with lower petrol consumption. The smaller van also fitted neatly into his drive and consequently was not a problem to neighbours. Disturbing neighbours is one of the key things to avoid if you are working from home.

Although moving house only a few miles, the move could have had a major impact on his trade. Steve gave this some careful thought and had a small leaflet printed with details of his new address and other changes. He sent these to all his existing customers. Steve did not think it appropriate to have mail or telephone calls redirected. The business did not suffer because of the move and Steve is at present happy with the way it has developed at his new home. Clearly, working from home and a mobile workshop imposes limitations on further growth. Larger jobs, particularly body repairs and paint spraying, are difficult. However, the current cost of even older premises makes it impossible to think of a more permanent workshop base.

Stewart Johnston

Stewart Johnston is currently a lecturer in architecture at a college of higher education in Scotland. As the architectural schools in colleges have been under threat in recent years, Stewart has begun to look increasingly outside higher education for his future livelihood. Stewart possesses skills as both a designer and an upholsterer and he anticipates developing one of these skills into a full-time business over the next two or three years.

Stewart's business interests have grown over a number of

years. At first they developed informally by word of mouth; in more recent years he has actively tried to build up customers and contacts to enable him to start in business on his own. This development has forced Stewart to adapt and change his working environment.

His architectural and design practice started simply by helping neighbours prepare plans for extensions and modifications to their houses. At that stage he felt no qualms about completing work at his college and using their facilities for drawing and copying. Over time this work increased as his neighbours told their friends and business associates of his skills. As the work took on an increasingly 'private' nature he felt that he could no longer use college facilities, so he purchased some second-hand drawing and computing equipment and set up business in his own converted loft at home. At first this was quite adequate as his clients were still friends of friends who accepted the climb to the top of his house, past bedrooms scattered with toys. But as clients came from increasingly tenuous links with his friends Stewart felt they expected a more professional environment in which to discuss their problems. Stewart was also aware of the domestic tension created by meeting clients at home. Children had to be 'silenced' during important telephone conversations. The loft which was converted some four years ago as their third child's bedroom was filled with equipment. Stewart needed an environment appropriate to his profession in which to meet his clients but did not want the costs of maintaining an office full time.

The short-term solution, at least until Stewart has a large enough client base to leave education and begin practice full time, has been found in a local country club. The small meeting rooms which the club possesses are available for business meetings at a cost of £5 per hour and provide an ideal prestigious venue for meeting clients. At first Stewart was worried about the availability of these rooms but he has found from experience that there is always space available when needed. He regards the membership cost of £170 per year, as a retainer on the room, one which both he and his family are happy to accept, as it gives the entire family access to the club's facilities.

Stewart's other skill as an upholsterer was gained in the course of renovating furniture for his own home. At present it is a hobby, but one which has brought in additional income by undertaking work for friends on an informal basis. He does, though, derive a great deal of personal satisfaction from this work. He buys items of furniture at local auctions to renovate and sell through local antique shops. Currently this is done on a very casual basis. Unfortunately, the collection and renovation of furniture takes a considerable amount of storage and workshop space. The garage is now full of furniture in various stages of renovation, while the family car remains out on the drive.

Stewart agrees that he is in the classic dilemma of many embryo businesses: too many ideas to be implemented successfully. However, he does like the stimulus of a variety of activities and finds it hard to be single-minded over one. Whichever of the two skills he develops into a full-time business, Stewart is aware that he will have to make decisions about premises. The design business can be continued using rooms in the country club and the loft at home, but the upholstery business will need more permanent premises than his garage. Stewart imagines that his neighbours would be far from happy to accommodate an upholstery business in their leafy estate.

Cedars Hotel

In July 1985 Clive Barley, Tony Carter and their respective families became the proprietors of the Cedars Hotel in Stowmarket. For both families the purchase of the Cedars Hotel, a freehold property, was the culmination of 15 months' searching for a suitable hotel to start up in business together. Before the purchase of the hotel, Mr Barley had been employed for more than 20 years by Guinness as a catering manager. Mr Carter was employed by the National Westminster Bank. Both families had been good friends for a number of years and after a lengthy period discussing ideas for a business venture they finally decided to start looking for premises in March 1984.

They had very clear and well developed ideas about the type of property they wanted. The main specifications were:

- A freehold property.
- A location in the south of England.
- A location in a flourishing town with growth potential.
- Adequate 'living in' accommodation for both families.
- Fifteen bedrooms or more so that there was adequate work for both families.
- Conference facilities.
- Dining facilities.
- Adequate car parking.
- Central heating.

119

The main sources of information which they consulted were the *Caterer and Hotelkeeper* magazine, local estate agents, and specialist agents dealing in hotels. It was this last source which provided the best selection of properties. Numerous properties were visited; some were poor, others provided very interesting possibilities. Mr Barley became particularly interested in one hotel in Wisbech in Cambridgeshire. First impressions of the hotel and a cursory look at the accounts and building seemed very promising. But a closer look at Wisbech convinced the two men that it was not an ideal location to develop the hotel venture. A couple of months later the hotel in Stowmarket came on the market and both families agreed that it satisfied most of the criteria which they had previously established.

The hotel was on Needham Road, the main A45 until the bypass was built, to the east of Stowmarket. It had 17 bed-rooms and adequate 'living in' accommodation for both families. As the initial examination was favourable they had a closer look at the previous owners' accounts. Mr Carter's banking experience was particularly helpful when examining the accounts. Even so, Mr Carter decided to seek the advice of a firm of accountants with experience in business purchase. The first firm he contacted left Mr Carter with the feeling that the venture was really too small for their interest so he turned to a second firm. This firm was far more helpful and willing to get involved in what was a major decision for both families.

Throughout negotiations the bank, which both families had joined, was kept informed of what they were doing. The bank manager was particularly helpful and regularly took time to discuss developments with the two families. Both families regarded his help as invaluable. When, after a thorough search of the detailed accounts, the accountants and bank manager had approved the business, a surveyor was engaged to examine the property. This was really a final check to ensure that the property was structurally sound. The survey cost approximately £800 but the information which it provided was useful in two ways. First, it provided a basis on which to negotiate the asking price down. Second, after purchase it provided a checklist of minor works which were required to maintain the property. Mr Carter believes that the old 'stitch in time' adage is relevant and the surveyor's fee has already paid for itself.

In March 1985 the two families made an offer for the

property and on 3 July 1985 they moved into the hotel, having sold their respective homes and borrowed some money from the bank. The hotel is already thriving. The two partners' catering and financial skills complement each other very well and plans are already under way to expand the hotel and provide more single bedrooms to cater for the influx of weekday businessmen who currently fill the hotel to capacity.

Peppercorn Wholefoods

Joan and Frank Savage began their health food business four years ago in a small town in the Home Counties. The original idea for the business came from Joan who had been looking for a new interest now that their three children were at school. Joan had always been interested in wholefoods in her own domestic cooking and had become quite an expert in her own right. The thought of her own business combining these interests appealed to both her and her husband. They thought that a retail business would fit in well with their domestic routine, as they could if necessary buy in assistance quite cheaply.

Between them, Joan and Frank put together a simple business plan, which demonstrated that their proposition was viable. The business they were proposing did not require a great deal of capital and could be financed from their own modest assets. Using their business plan as ammunition, they persuaded their bank manager to grant a small overdraft to cover day-to-day requirements.

Joan had given some thought to buying the stock and goodwill of a going concern. However, it rapidly became clear that as there were no other health food outlets in their local area (domestic commitments would not permit long journeys to work), she would have to look around for vacant property. Never having run a business before, Joan admitted to being very naive about property. She visited several agents to gain background information on the local retail property market. After some weeks' searching and waiting for an appropriate property to come on to the market, a shop became available locally in a small side street about 50 or 60 yards from the main shopping centre. The property had a sales area of approximately 300 square feet with a small back room for storage. The shop was offered on a seven-year lease, of which three years had yet to run. The previous tenant from whom Joan was indirectly buying the lease had had to give up the business because of ill health. That was the explanation given by the agent. Joan did not consider checking this story. Neither Joan nor her solicitor were concerned that the lease had only three years left to run as it was generally assumed that renewal would be no problem.

Frank and a colleague helped fit the new shop with appropriate shelving and gave it a quick coat of emulsion paint ready for opening. When the shop opened it provided Joan with the challenge she required, but it did not produce the turnover which had been anticipated despite there being no other competition in the town. This, Joan suggests, was due to her failure to undertake any serious market research. From her growing experiences she realised that health food trade in the town was divided into two groups, the regular serious trade and the casual trade. For the former group her location in a side street was not important. However, for the casual shopper she was 'off the beaten track' so she missed this very valuable additional trade. A second problem was the amount of space; the 300 square feet of selling space had very high ceilings, and the level of stock she could afford to carry made the space look relatively empty. Consequently the image created was of a quiet shop with limited stock.

The bombshell came when Joan read in a local paper that the row of shops in which she had her business was to be demolished and redeveloped by a local property company which had bought the freehold from her landlord. Immediate contact with the agent and her solicitor confirmed that this was the case and that the lease, which had over 15 months to run, would not be renewed. It subsequently transpired that the previous tenant had been forewarned of this development and had relocated his business rather than retiring. While her solicitor advised that it would be possible to fight the redevelopment in association with other tenants in the area, Joan decided that she just did not want the hassle and uncertainty involved. A new site was the only answer.

A lot had been learned in the Savage household about retailing by now and both Joan and Frank were much clearer about their accommodation needs. Although the business had not been a massive success they were both still convinced that they should continue.

Two factors were uppermost in their minds when they began to look for alternative premises. First, the size and layout of the selling area were crucial. An area of 150 to 200 square feet would be quite adequate for the stocks which Joan intended to carry. A small store room would be useful, but not essential. Second, the shop must be located so as to take advantage of casual trade.

After looking at several properties which were vacant, they decided on a unit in a new parade of shops just off the main street, which was *en route* to the town's main car park. The shop was certainly upmarket from the previous one and this was reflected in the rental, just less than double the price per unit area. However, the shop was considerably smaller, with approximately 160 square feet of selling area, so that the total rental was about the same. The rateable value was also higher. The new shop was more efficient, easier to clean and cheaper to heat and light. The property was taken on a five-year lease.

While the move was only over a short distance, less than a quarter of a mile, Joan took the trouble to plan and publicise it carefully. The local paper had been interested in the re-development scheme and had run an article earlier in which the plight of the tenants had been a central issue. They were now more than happy to do a feature on Joan and her new shop. Two of her suppliers agreed to insert 'good luck' adverts in the paper the week the new shop opened.

Joan arranged with the Post Office to redirect her mail for a six-month period. She also retained her former telephone number as the move was within the same exchange.

The move itself was undertaken over a weekend and was very much a family occasion. The family estate car provided the transport and the three children willing labour. By Monday morning the new shop was ready for business. When the Savages had finished their second shopfitting contract they were well experienced and the shop looked very attractive. Joan began to see how important space and layout can be in retailing. With three or four customers in the shop it now gave the appearance of a very busy successful business.

Trade has increased progressively. Joan has noticed the extent to which casual trade has increased. Shoppers on their way to and from the main car park frequently stop and look in the well-presented window. Attracted by what they see, many come in and make purchases.

Joan and Frank are now very happy with their business. They are philosophical about their initial problems and are more than aware of their naivety about business and property. They now feel they have found an ideal property which suits the business they want to develop.

General, Marine and Life

Tim Ingram's experience is in many ways a microcosm of the world of small business. Disenchantment with working for a large organisation, starting up on a part-time basis, working initially from home and then moving to business premises are all standard ingredients in the development of small firms. In addition, Tim's story incorporates a number of more individual elements including a move from London to Plymouth, a failed partnership and an estate management function as landlord to a number of small subtenants.

In the late 1960s Tim was assistant district manager for the Co-operative Insurance Society Ltd (CIS), working at its Palmers Green branch in North London. He was a successful and secure employee in a large and respected company, but the job was not satisfying. In particular Tim was frustrated by the lack of scope and discretion open to him and by the limited range of policies he was able to offer to clients. As a result he became increasingly attracted by the idea of setting up in broking, and in 1969 he established General, Marine and Life. The business started operations at home on the dining room table, with Tim retaining his full-time position with the Co-op and working for himself in the evenings and at weekends. The experiment proved successful and within a year a decision had been made to head towards full-time self-employment.

As part of this major review of future plans, Tim and his wife Shirley, also decided to leave London. Big cities, like big companies, were not to their liking and so they looked instead for a place offering a more attractive environment as well as good business prospects. Their choice of Plymouth was encouraged by previous holidays in the area and by Tim's interest in all things maritime, including not only marine insurance but also his favourite recreation, under-water diving. They believed that Plymouth offered good commercial prospects. Tim sensed that the town was likely to expand, as indeed it has.

There was only one serious obstacle to overcome in this progression to self-employment. Moving and buying a new house would require a mortgage but the building societies would be sceptical about financing someone just about to become self-employed. The answer, as an interim arrangement, was to look for a post in the Plymouth area with an established insurance company. By obtaining a position with the Plymouth branch of Colonial Mutual Life Tim secured a job, an introduction to the local insurance community and a building society mortgage for a three-bedroomed bungalow on the city's eastern edge. For Colonial Mutual Life Tim acted as a life insurance salesman: in his spare time he concentrated on other kinds of insurance for his own firm, General, Marine and Life, 90 per cent of whose original clients are still with Tim today despite his 200 mile move.

After a year of building up the business, turnover had grown to the point where it was possible to leave Colonial Mutual Life and to become wholly self-employed. There was no money, however, for specialist premises and the business was run from the bungalow (without troubling to ask about planning permission). Tim recalls only too well the problems of trying to combine a domestic and a commercial life under one roof. At meal times the 'office desk' reverted to being the dining room table and all the paper-work had to be cleared away. The telephone would ring at all hours of the day and clients would call without warning and at the least convenient times. The two young children, David and Karen, would come and sit on daddy's lap while policies were being written up and costs calculated. The sound of the children's voices, cheers and tears, would submerge telephone calls and discussions with clients in the dining room.

The one advantage of being at home was that Shirley was able to act as secretary and typist. But inevitably as the business grew the clerical tasks became too large for Shirley to cope with and so two part-time girls were employed at the bungalow as secretaries and bookkeepers. The neighbours gossiped about these two young ladies calling every day and eventually it was the attention of neighbours which brought this phase of the business to an end. The lady in the bungalow next door, in discussion with Tim on another property issue, pointedly brought to his attention that the deeds of her property clearly prohibited its use for business purposes. There was no explicit pressure but the message was clear enough: encouraged by this veiled threat the hunt for premises began.

The search was undertaken by talking to business contacts and by checking the property advertisements in the local newspapers. The overriding consideration was to find somewhere cheap as the whole exercise had to be conducted on a shoe-string. Eventually a room was found, costing, including rates, about £50 a month (at mid-70s prices). It was on the

125

top floor of 40 New Street, a 300-year-old building in the Barbican area, about 200 yards from Sutton Pool and the Mayflower Steps, the famous departure point of the Pilgrim Fathers. New Street is narrow and quiet and, apart from summer tourists, the pedestrian flows are low; but given that the insurance business does not depend on a passing trade this was not too serious a problem. Indeed, the area's maritime traditions could even convey some advantage for marine insurance work.

In taking on the premises as a subtenant, there was no legal contract, only an exchange of letters with the leaseholder. In order to save money Tim fitted the office out and did the interior decoration work himself. This one small room at the top of a narrow staircase accommodated Tim, a full-time secretary, a part-time bookkeeper and all the files and furnishings. With space limited, one 'cottage industry' assistant was also employed working on a part-time basis in her own home.

After a year the leaseholders announced a 50 per cent rent increase and so General, Marine and Life was on the move again — but not far. Further along New Street the top floor of No 36 was vacant and so with minimal disruption the business moved eastwards 30 yards. A lease was taken out on all five top floor rooms, two being sublet to friends until the landlord objected and had them evicted. Shortly afterwards Tim obtained the lease on the entire building at a cost of about £8,000. This provided security of tenure for the remaining eight years on the lease and allowed the business to transfer to the ground floor which was more convenient both for clients and staff. Two of the three rooms were used for secretarial and reception purposes, leaving one office for Tim's personal use and as a private room for discussion with clients.

The current rental for the whole building is about £220 a month (excluding rates). The income from the four subtenants goes a long way towards meeting the bill but at various times in the past Tim's income has been reduced both by periods of voids and in one case by a subtenant's failure to pay the rent due — a frustrating and protracted saga.

Over the years the business has grown and prospered and it now employs two full-time and two part-time secretaries plus the 'out-worker'. The only really difficult period came when, as a result of expansion, Tim took on a partner who left four years later to go his own way. The business suffered disruption and a loss of clientele which took time to replace.

126

With the benefit of hindsight Tim feels that he should have attached more stringent conditions to the partnership and is now keen to advise others of their importance.

In looking to the future, the lease on 36 New Street expires next year. Until the cost and terms of the new lease are clear, Tim has no definite property plans. However, after more than ten years in rented premises he is attracted by the idea of owner-occupation. A series of complicated and unfortunate experiences with leases, landlords, subtenants and prodigiously slow solicitors has served to underline the advantages of having a place of your own — security, simplicity and an appreciating financial asset. Having graduated from working at home, through rented premises, Tim is now beginning to contemplate the next step up the property ladder.

Leyland Industrial Cases

Leyland Golley is a packing case manufacturer in his early fifties operating from what was originally a wool depot in the tiny Cornish village of Grampound Road midway between Truro and St Austell. The village is close to Cornwall's china clay country with views across to the white alps of the mining waste tips. Leyland is a Cornishman by birth but only returned to the Duchy in January 1984 when he moved his business over 300 miles from its previous location in Bolton, Lancashire.

Like many other small business owners Leyland has over the years tried his hand at all kinds of trades, sometimes working for others, sometimes working for himself. He has, for example, been employed as a trainee butler for a Siamese prince and princess, as a china clay miner, as an aerodrome fireman and as a mechanic for a wagon-building firm. For the last 20 years he has been self-employed, first as a builder and decorator, then as a producer of models of horses and carts, and most recently as a manufacturer of packing cases for the computer industry. His businesses have operated in a variety of environments including space at home (without notifying the planning authorities), a number of lock-up garages and part of a redundant textile mill.

Leyland started his present firm about ten years ago when cheap Spanish imports killed his model-making business. A friend in computer engineering drew his attention to the industry's need for carefully designed packing cases, often to individual specifications. Damage to items such as printed circuit boards, disc packs and visual display units can prove very expensive and so good quality cases are important. Leyland, ever adaptable, grasped the opportunity. The business was run from a rented cellar in a dilapidated Bolton mill. The premises, about 2,000 square feet, were cheap but, initially at least, were in an appalling condition. Leyland's previous experience in the building and decorating trade was therefore put to good use making the place habitable — illustrating again that when taking on old cheap premises it helps to be practically minded or at least to have an interest in DIY.

Why then was it decided to leave the refurbished cellar in Bolton and to move to Cornwall? In addition to the obvious environmental benefits, the answer was 'roots'. With fond childhood memories and continuing family ties in Cornwall, Leyland was keen to get back home. His wife had relatively few family connections in her home area around Bolton and once their two children, born and bred in Lancashire, had 'left the nest', the time was right for the long-planned move south. Moreover, with the business being operated single-handed, there were no employee problems to consider.

The absence of a commercial motive behind a long-distance move of this type is not unusual. Few small businesses are aware of particular trading opportunities in far-away places and hence long moves are often undertaken for other purposes. Nonetheless, in planning such moves every effort must be made not to damage the business, and in Leyland's case checks were made with his major customers (in different parts of the country) in order to gauge their attitude to the proposed reloation. The unanimous answer was that, providing prices and delivery times were unaffected, where the work was done was of no concern.

The search for premises was undertaken while on holiday in Cornwall. Leyland was unaware of the assistance which local authorities can offer in finding premises, so he relied exclusively on estate agents. The security and financial advantages of owner-occupation, together with a history of disagreements with a previous landlord, led to a strong preference for somewhere to buy. Several premises were visited. The main distinguishing feature of the site chosen (about 3,000 square feet) at Grampound Road, was an attractive asking price.

The move was accomplished with minimal disruption: existing customers were retained while, more recently, new locally based clients have been added. Operating from a remote area like the Cornish peninsula has posed relatively few problems. Customers send in drawings of their specifications by post and any queries are dealt with by telephone. In delivering the finished cases to clients, the carriers have agreed to charge the same fees as they applied in Bolton. In Leyland's experience the only difficulty of operating in such an isolated area is that he can no longer rely on quick, locally available sources of inputs and services: his response has been to do more jobs for himself and to increase his levels of self-sufficiency.

One final ingredient of the move is that Leyland has turned from being a tenant into being a landlord. He uses about 2,000 square feet of his premises for his own business and the remainder is rented out to another small firm. Moreover, this pattern is destined to grow. Leyland has already bought and refurbished an adjacent small property for renting out and is now starting to build three new units at the rear. In this initiative the local planners, keen to promote small businesses in a remote region with high unemployment, have been particularly helpful.

Within a year or so Leyland hopes, therefore, to have a total of four tenants. His current rental charges are about £1.60 (excluding rates) and by keeping his rents appreciably below his rivals (such as CoSIRA and English Estates), he is confident of finding the new tenants he will need. This new role of property developer is especially important in Leyland's long-term plans. When he retires, he intends to retain ownership of his premises and use their rents as a continuing source of income to provide for a more comfortable retirement. As this example shows, premises can be productive in more ways than one.

Allen Priest and Sons Ltd

The building now occupied by Allen Priest and Sons Ltd was owned by a family controlled textile company for 200 years until the company went into liquidation in 1982. In order to maintain the family tradition in textiles one member of the family set up a new company, Allen Priest and Sons Ltd, to manufacture textile machinery. The mill was bought as a manufacturing base and was regarded as an excellent investment. The intention was to occupy some of the building for manufacturing purposes and to subdivide and let the remainder for small businesses, thereby providing simple diversification for the company.

129

The three-storey, 48,000 square foot mill was built in the late nineteenth century, with some more buildings being added during this century. The overall condition of the mill was very good as it had been maintained to a very high standard. Facilities in the building when purchased included electricity, gas, water and a full sprinkler system.

The company had no experience in property development prior to purchasing the building. One of the directors was, however, a maintenance engineer and he proved to be a very useful member of the team when alterations were undertaken. Advice about subdividing the mill was sought from local estate agents who advised on a firm of architects to employ for the design work. They also later helped to market the property. The subdivision work was self-managed by the owners. The major part of the work was put out to tender to local builders. Some selective demolition was carried out to provide more car parking space, but the major work was in partitioning and refurbishing the subdivided units. Facilities now provided to each unit include electricity, gas and water. Electricity is supplied from a central switchboard and units have their own meter (the cost of installing meters is borne by the tenants). Toilet and washing facilities are available in each unit.

Only months before the former occupiers ceased trading, they had installed a new oil fired central heating system to the entire property. Priests were reluctant to dismantle this system so it has been used to heat the newly subdivided units. Unfortunately, such a system is difficult to administer in the small units and the allocation of heating charges to individual tenants has caused some difficulties.

Some internal rebuilding has been required to meet fire regulations. Corridors have been built to provide protected areas and a means of escape. All units are divided by 9-inch breeze block walls. Access to all units on the ground floor is good and the selective demolition of parts of the property has provided adequate parking space for 20 cars.

Fourteen units have been completed at the development. One is currently used by Allen Priest and Sons Ltd for production of textile machinery. Other units are occupied by a variety of companies. These include textile manufacturers, metal engineers, a decorating business, shopfitters, and a cash and carry wholesalers. Units vary in size from 500 to 8,000 square feet, the average being about 3,400 square feet. Annual income from the occupied units is now £60,000.

The company is very pleased with this return on their investment. The total cost of subdividing the building was about £90,000. Because the building was bought relatively cheaply from liquidators and was subdivided economically, the company will achieve a payback in under four years.

All tenants have three-year lease agreements at a rental of £1.50 per square foot. Upper-storey units with slightly more difficult access were the last to be occupied and had to be offered at a lower rental level. Each tenant insures the contents of their own unit separately. All tenancies are managed by a local firm of estate agents. Allen Priest and Sons Ltd have found this a very satisfactory arrangement since they can concentrate on developing their own manufacturing business without worrying about the day-to-day administration of their property. They have found that the subdivision of the property has provided sufficient funds for them to develop their own business.

The property has also been excellent security against which their bankers have provided loans to develop the new textile manufacturing business. One of the directors of Allen Priest and Sons Ltd was a member of the firm which previously owned the property. He strongly believes that if the previous company had realised the amount of unused space they possessed and the possibilities offered by subdivision, they would probably have been able to save their company from collapse.

Cox, Wilcox and Company

Trevor Jones's metal goods manufacturing company, Cox, Wilcox and Company, has suffered periods of failure as well as success. In 1977 it employed 85 people and exported to countries all over the world, in particular to the USA. Now it employs only 15. In the same period output has decreased and most of the company's export markets have been lost. The only major success for Mr Jones, the managing director, was to realise several years ago that his business was failing.

In 1978 he took two days off work to determine what the future held in store for his company. The business, typical of many of the 'metal bashers' in the West Midlands, was suffering at the hands of cheap foreign imports and a general fall in demand resulting from the recession. On a sales trip to Australia and New Zealand in the summer of 1978, Mr Jones took the opportunity of stopping off in the Far East. Here he saw a highly competitive metal industry, based on cheap labour,

131

which was rapidly taking over markets traditionally the preserve of West Midlands companies. On the basis of what he found he realised that within the foreseeable future his trading position could only worsen. He decided to act quickly. He reduced the number of manufactured products and much to his regret made severe reductions in the size of his workforce in order to increase productivity. Despite all his best efforts to compete more effectively, his company's market position and profit margins continued their ever downward spiral. Having used the major proportion of surplus funds to keep the company trading, he realised that the only remaining asset was the factory itself. Although he had no experience of property development he decided that the only way of saving the company was to diversify and somehow make use of the 29,000 square foot single-storey building which the company owned.

The company's reduction in output and smaller workforce meant that large, but dispersed, areas of the factory were unused. He therefore decided to consolidate the company's machinery into a smaller area. Mr Jones realised that concentration of production in a small area could help to reduce the company's overheads of heating and lighting but that although these savings were beneficial, the major costs were rates, insurance and maintenance. He decided that the only way to avoid these and gain financial income from the property would be to subdivide the premises into small business units. Rates, insurance and maintenance costs would then be paid by the tenants. The rental income from the subdivided units would ensure that previously unused areas of the factory were again providing a financial contribution to the company.

Mr Jones hoped that the funds generated from renting the vacant floor space could be used to finance the future expansion of the company. In the event the company was further affected by the general decline in the metal goods industry. While many of his previous competitors and friends went out of business he was able to survive by expanding the property development side of his business.

With the help of friends in the property business, architects, building inspectors and his bank manager, Mr Jones developed plans which evaluated the potential subdivision of the whole building. The plans served a dual purpose: they gave the company a structured but flexible route for contraction, while at the same time defining areas which could be most easily subdivided into new units. All machinery was moved by the company's own employees during weekends and at other times when production was slack, ensuring that normal production was not affected. Some of the employees were also involved in the installation of new electricity meters and power points to the new units.

The first four units were completed in 1980. Breeze block walls were constructed to subdivide the units and new entrances were provided using household garage doors. The units had an average size of 2,000 square feet and were fully self-contained with their own office and toilet facilities. Initially, access to each of these units was provided by a narrow passageway. Problems with this restricted access route and a lack of nearby car parking space for the new tenants was overcome when Mr Jones bought two adjoining houses next door to the factory. The gardens to the rear of these houses were over 200 feet long and ran parallel to the passageway. By reducing the gardens to only 20 feet, the remaining area provided improved access to the units and additional car parking space.

Subsequently the company developed an additional three 2,000 square foot units in the remainder of the property. In contrast to the previous four units, these units were subdivided at practically no cost. They were based on existing areas within the factory. No additional facilities were provided and the tenants in these three units share washing and toilet facilities with Mr Jones's company. Separate access routes to the units could not be provided and tenants share an entrance to the building with Cox, Wilcox and Company. Although a little inconvenient at times, all the companies concerned seem happy with the situation.

All tenancies are managed by Mr Jones who is available on site at all times. Tenants in the four self-contained units which were completed first have three-year leases. These require all repairs to be carried out by the tenants and stipulate that interior redecoration and exterior painting is undertaken every three years. All of these tenants had an initial 18-month rental of £1.00 per square foot to enable them to carry out alterations to their units. Subsequently, rents rose to £2.00 per square foot. The remaining units, which share access and other facilities with Cox, Wilcox and Company, do not have formal leases. Instead they have a 'gentlemen's agreement'. They have lower rentals of £1.20 per square foot reflecting the inconvenience of shared access and services. Tenants in these units

HOW TO CHOOSE BUSINESS PREMISES

also share bills with the owner, whereas other units have separately metered and billed services. Insurance and rates on the building are paid for by the owner. Tenants' contributions to this are determined by the proportion of square footage occupied. All tenants have their own insurance for goods and machinery.

When asked to look back over the development process and review the pros and cons of such a diversification, Mr Jones felt that one of the most important issues was to have realised the potential of subdivision so early in his own manufacturing company's decline. He strongly believes that if subdivision had not been undertaken his company would have ceased trading some time ago. He subdivided at a time when the market for premises was buoyant and rents were still relatively high. The returns on his investment have therefore been maintained at a high level over the three years that the majority of leases have run. He has already recognised that these levels may not be maintained in the future. Mr Jones believes that it is important to develop a good relationship with tenants so that difficulties and differences can be resolved amicably. The only major problem encountered was when one of his tenants became bankrupt and he had difficulty in repossessing the property from the liquidators. He eventually had to take the case to court. With the value of hindsight he believes he should, perhaps, have stuck more strongly to the clause in his leases which allows immediate repossession of property once rents are more than one month overdue.

The enterprise which Mr Jones has shown in diversifying his company's activities demonstrates how a failing business can once again become successful by subdividing its property.

Appendices

Useful Addresses

Council for Small Industries in Rural Areas (CoSIRA)

NATIONAL HEADQUARTERS
AND WILTSHIRE OFFICE

141 Castle Street
Salisbury
Wiltshire SP1 3TP
0722 336255

COUNTY OFFICES

209 Redland Road
Bristol
Avon BS6 6XU
0272 733433

Agriculture House
55 Goldington Road
Bedford MK40 3LU
0234 61381

24 Brooklands Avenue
Cambridge CB2 2BU
0223 354505

6 Shropshire Street
Audlem
Cheshire CW3 0DY
0270 812012

Highshore House
New Bridge Street
Truro
Cornwall TR1 1AA
0872 73531

Ullswater Road
Penrith
Cumbria CA1 7EH
0768 68752

Agricola House
Church Street
Wirksworth
Derbyshire DE4 4EY
062 982 4848

27 Victoria Park Road
Exeter
Devon EX2 4NT
0392 52616

Room 12/13 Wing D
Government Buildings
Prince of Wales Road
Dorchester
Dorset DT1 1QJ
0305 68558

Morton Road
Darlington
Co Durham DL1 4PT
0325 487123

Sussex House
212 High Street
Lewes
East Sussex BN7 2NH
0273 471339

BEES Small Business Centre
Hay Lane
Braintree
Essex CM7 6ST
0376 47623

Northgate Place
Staple Gardens
Winchester
Hants SO23 8SR
0962 54747

14 Market Place
Howden
Goole
Humberside DN14 7BJ
0430 31138

6-7 Town Lane
Newport
Isle of Wight PO30 1JU
0983 528019

8 Romney Place
Maidstone
Kent ME15 6LE
0622 65222

15 Victoria Road
Fulwood
Preston
Lancs PR2 4PS
0772 713038

Council Offices
Eastgate
Sleaford
Lincs NG34 7EB
0529 303241

12 Unthank Road
Norwich
Norfolk NR2 2PA
0603 624498

Hunsbury Hill Farm
Rothersthorpe Road
Northampton
Northants NN4 9QX
0604 65874

Northumberland Business Centre
Southgate
Morpeth
Northumberland NE61 2EH
0670 58807

William House
Shipton Road
Skelton
York
North Yorkshire YO3 6WZ
0904 646866

Chancel House
East Street
Bingham
Notts NG13 8DR
0949 39222

The Maltings
St John's Road
Wallingford
Oxon OX10 9BZ
0491 35523

Strickland House
The Lawns
Park Street
Telford
Shropshire TF1 3BX
0952 47161

1 The Crescent
Taunton
Somerset TA1 4EA
0823 76905

12 Churchfields Court
Barnsley
South Yorkshire S70 2JT
0226 204367

Bridge Street
Hadleigh
Nr Ipswich
Suffolk IP7 6BY
0473 827893

2 Jenner Road
Guildford
Surrey GU1 3PN
0483 38385

The Abbotsford
10 Market Place
Warwick
Warwickshire CV34 4SL
0926 499593

32 Church Street
Malvern
Worcs WR14 2AZ
068 45 64506

Department of Trade and Industry

CENTRAL AND REGIONAL OFFICES

1 Victoria Street
London SW1
01-215 7877

Birmingham

Ladywood House
Stephenson Street
Birmingham B2 4DT
021-632 4111

Bristol

The Pithay
Bristol
Avon BS1 2NB
0272 272666

Leeds

Priestley House
Park Row
Leeds LS1 5SF
0532 443171

London

Charles House
375 Kensington High Street
London W14 8QM
01-603 2060

Manchester

Sunley Building
Piccadilly Plaza
Manchester M1 4BA
061-236 2171

Newcastle

Stanegate House
2 Groat Market
Newcastle upon Tyne NE1 1YN
0632 324722

Nottingham

Severns House
20 Middle Pavement
Nottingham
NG1 7DW
0602 506181

Department of Employment, Small Firms Service

All centres can be contacted by dialling 100 and asking for Freefone Enterprise

Headquarters

Ashdown House
123 Victoria Street
London SW1 6RB
01-212 5946

Birmingham

6th Floor
Ladywood House
Stephenson Street
Birmingham B2 4DT
021-643 3344

Bristol

5th Floor
The Pithay
Bristol
Avon BS1 2NB
0272 294546

Cambridge

24 Brooklands Avenue
Cambridge CB2 2BU
0223 63312

Cardiff

16 St David's House
Wood Street
Cardiff
S Glam CF1 1ER
0222 396116

Glasgow

120 Bothwell Street
Glasgow G2 7JP
041-248 6014

Leeds

1 Park Row
City Square
Leeds LS1 5NR
0532 445151

Liverpool
Graeme House
Derby Square
Liverpool L2 7UJ
051-236 5756

London
Ebury Bridge House
2-18 Ebury Bridge Road
London SW1W 8QD
01-730 8451

Manchester
3rd Floor
320-325 Royal Exchange Buildings
St Ann's Square
Manchester M2 7AH
061-832 5282

Newcastle
Centro House
3 Cloth Market
Newcastle upon Tyne NE1 3EE
0632 325353

Nottingham
Severns House
20 Middle Pavement
Nottingham NG1 7DW
0602 581205

Reading
Abbey Hall
Abbey Square
Reading
Berks RG1 3BE
0734 591733

English Estates

St George's House
Kingsway
Team Valley
Gateshead
Tyne and Wear NE11 0NA
0632 878941

Bodmin
53 Fore Street
Bodmin
Cornwall PL31 2JB
0208 3631

Doncaster
Hallgate House
19 Hallgate
Doncaster DN1 3NN
0302 66865

Liverpool
Sandon House
157 Regent Road
Liverpool L5 9TF
051-933 2020

Thornaby
Forster House
Allensway
Thornaby
Cleveland TS17 9HA
0642 765911

Workington
Salterbeck Industrial Estate
Workington
Cumbria CA14 5DX
0946 830469

Health and Safety Executive Area Offices

South West
Inter City House
Mitchell Lane
Victoria Street
Bristol BS1 6AN
0272 290681

South
Priestley House
Priestley Road
Basingstoke RG24 9NW
0256 3181

South East
3 Grinstead House
London Road
East Grinstead
West Sussex RH19 1RR
0342 26922

London North West
Chancel House
Neasden Lane
London NW10 2UD
01-459 8855

London North East
Maritime House
1 Linton Road
Barking
Essex G11 8HF
01-594 5522

London South
1 Long Lane
London SE1 4PG
01-407 8911

East Anglia
39 Baddow Road
Chelmsford CM2 0HL
0245 84661

Northern Home Counties
14 Cardiff Road
Luton LU1 1PP
0582 34121

East Midlands
5th Floor
Belgrave House
Greyfriars
Northampton NN1 2BS
0604 21233

West Midlands
McLaren Building
2 Masshouse Circus
Queensway
Birmingham B4 7NP
021-236 5080

Wales
Brunel House
2 Fitzalan Road
Cardiff CF2 1SH
0222 497777

Marches
The Marches House
Midway, Newcastle under Lyme
Staffs ST5 1DT
0782 610181

North Midlands
Birbeck House
Trinity Square
Nottingham NG1 4AU
0602 40712

South Yorkshire and Humberside
Sovereign House
40 Silver Street
Sheffield S1 2ES
0742 739081

West and North Yorkshire
8 St Paul's Street
Leeds LS1 2LE
0532 446191

Greater Manchester
Quay House
Quay Street
Manchester M3 3JB
061-831 7111

Merseyside
The Triad
Stanley Road
Bootle
Merseyside L20 3PG
051-922 7211

North West
Victoria House
Ormskirk Road
Preston PR1 1HH
0722 59321

North East
Government Buildings
Kenton Bar
Newcastle upon Tyne NE1 2YX
0632 869811

Scotland East
Belford House
59 Belford Road
Edinburgh EH4 3UE
031-225 1313

Scotland West
314 St Vincent Street
Glasgow G3 8XG
041-204 2646

Other useful addresses

BSC Industry Ltd
NLA Tower
12 Addiscombe Road
Croydon CR9 3JH
01-686 0366

British Technology Group
101 Newington Causeway
London SE1 6BU
01-403 6666

British Technology Group North
9 Hunters Mews
Wilmslow
Cheshire SK9 2AR
0625 532343

British Technology Group Scotland
87 St Vincent Street
Glasgow G2 5TF
041-221 1820

Business in the Community
227a City Road
London EC1V 1JU
01-253 3716

Development Board for Rural Wales
Ladywell House
Newtown
Powys SY16 1JB
0686 26965

Development Commission
11 Cowley Street
London SW1P 3NA
01-222 9134

EUROPEAN COAL AND STEEL
COMMUNITY

Details of loans: in England from
regional offices of the Department
of Trade and Industry or Regional
Support, Inward Investment and
Tourism Division

Kingsgate House
66-74 Victoria Street
London SW1E 6SJ
01-212 0814

In Wales, Investment Department:
Welsh Development Agency
Pearl House
Greyfriars Road
Cardiff CF1 3XF
0222 32955

In Scotland, Industry Department
for Scotland:
Alhambra House
45 Waterloo Street
Glasgow G2 6AT
041-248 2855

In Northern Ireland:
Department of Economic
Development
EC Branch
Netherleigh
Massey Avenue
Belfast BT4 2JP
0232 63244

NCB ENTERPRISE LTD,
AREA OFFICES

Scotland

Greenpark
Greenend
Liberton
Edinburgh EH17 7PZ
031-664 1461

North East

Coal House
Team Valley
Gateshead
Tyne and Wear NE11 0JD
091 4878822

North Yorkshire

PO Box 13
Allerton Bywater
Castleford WF12 2AL
0977 556511

Doncaster

St George's
Thorn Road
Doncaster DN1 2JS
0302 66733

Barnsley

Grimethorpe
Nr Barnsley S72 7AB
0226 710000

South Yorkshire

Wath upon Dearne
Nr Rotherham S63 7EW
0709 873331

Western

Staffordshire House
Berry Hill Road
Fenton
Stoke-on-Trent ST4 2NH
0782 48201

North Derbyshire

Bolsover
Nr Chesterfield S44 6AA
0246 822231

North Nottinghamshire

Edwinstowe
Mansfield
Nottinghamshire NG21 9PR

South Nottinghamshire

Bestwood
Nottingham NG6 8UE
0602 273711

South Midlands

Coleorton Hall
Coleorton
Leicester LE6 4FA
0533 413131

South Wales

Coal House
Llanishen
Cardiff CF4 5YS
0222 753232

Kent

1-3 Waterloo Crescent
Dover
0304 201401

Northern Ireland Local Enterprise
Development Unit (LEDU)
LEDU House
Upper Galwally
Belfast BT8 4TB
0232 691031

Northern Ireland Industrial
Development Board
IDB House
64 Chichester Street
Belfast BT1 4JX
0232 234488/233233

Scottish Business in the
Community
Eagle Star House
St Andrew Square
Edinburgh
031-556 9761

Scottish Development Agency
120 Bothwell Street
Glasgow G2 7JP
041-248 2700

Scottish Office
New St Andrew's House
St James' Centre
Edinburgh
Lothian EH1 3SX
031-556 8400

Welsh Development Agency
Treforest Industrial Estate
Pontypridd
Mid Glam CF37 5UT
044 385 2666

Welsh Office
Cathays Park
Cardiff
St Glam CF1 3NQ
0222 825111

Areas of Government Assistance

Inner city areas

PARTNERSHIP AREAS

Birmingham
Hackney
Islington
Lambeth
Liverpool
Manchester/Salford
Newcastle/Gateshead

PROGRAMME AUTHORITIES

Blackburn
Bolton
Bradford
Brent
Coventry
Hammersmith and Fulham
Kingston upon Hull
Knowsley
Leeds
Leicester
Middlesbrough
North Tyneside
Nottingham
Oldham
Rochdale
Sandwell
Sheffield
South Tyneside
Sunderland
Tower Hamlets
Wandsworth
Wirral
Wolverhampton

OTHER DISTRICTS WHERE UDG BIDS CAN BE MADE

Barnsley
Burnley

Doncaster
Ealing
Greenwich
Harringay
Hartlepool
Langbaurgh
Lewisham
Newham
Rotherham
St Helens
Sefton
Southwark
Walsall
Wigan

Assisted Areas

(Assisted Areas are based on 'travel to work' areas)

DEVELOPMENT AREAS

England

North West
    Liverpool
    Widnes and Runcorn
    Wigan and St Helens
    Wirral and Chester
    Workington

North East
    Bishop Auckland
    Hartlepool
    Middlesbrough
    Newcastle upon Tyne
    South Tyneside
    Stockton-on-Tees
    Sunderland

Yorkshire and Humberside
  Rotherham and Mexborough
  Scunthorpe
  Whitby

East Midlands
  Corby

South West
  Falmouth
  Helston
  Newquay
  Penzance and St Ives
  Redruth and Camborne

Scotland

Arbroath
Bathgate
Cumnock and Sanquhar
Dumbarton
Dundee
Glasgow
Greenock
Irvine
Kilmarnock
Lanarkshire

Wales

Aberdare
Cardigan
Ebbw Vale and Abergavenny
Flint and Rhyl
Holyhead
Lampeter and Aberaeron
Merthyr and Rhymney
Neath and Port Talbot
Pontypridd and Rhondda
South Pembrokeshire
Wrexham

INTERMEDIATE AREAS

England

North West
  Accrington and Rossendale
  Blackburn
  Bolton and Bury
  Part of Manchester
  Oldham
  Rochdale

North East
  Darlington
  Durham
  Morpeth and Ashington

Yorkshire and Humberside
  Barnsley
  Bradford
  Doncaster
  Grimsby
  Hull
  Sheffield

West Midlands
  Birmingham
  Coventry and Hinckley
  Dudley and Sandwell
  Kidderminster
  Telford and Bridgnorth
  Walsall
  Wolverhampton

East Midlands
  Gainsborough

South West
  Bodmin and Liskeard
  Bude
  Cinderford and Ross-on-Wye
  Plymouth

Scotland

Ayr
Alloa
Badenoch
Campbeltown
Dunfermline
Dunoon and Bute
Falkirk
Forres
Girvan
Invergordon and Dingwall
Kirkcaldy
Lochaber
Newton Stewart
Skye and Wester Ross
Stewartry
Stranraer
Sutherland
Western Isles
Wick

Wales

Bangor and Caernarfon
Bridgend
Cardiff
Fishguard
Haverfordwest
Llanelli
Newport
Pontypool and Cwmbran
Porthmadoc and Ffestiniog
Pwllheli
Swansea

Enterprise Zones

Belfast

Belfast Enterprise Zone Office
Adelaide Street
Belfast BT2 8NR
0232 248449

Clydebank

Development Officer
Clydebank Task Force
Clyde House
170 Kilbowie Road
Clydebank
041-952 0084

Corby

Director of Industry
Corby Industrial Development
Centre
Douglas House
Queens Square
Corby
Northants NN17 1PL
05366 62571

Delyn

Delyn Borough Council
Enterprise House
Aber Park
Flint
Clwyd
03526 4004

Dudley

Industrial Development Unit
Council House
Dudley
West Midlands DY1 1HF
0384 55433

Glanford

Glanford Borough Council
Council Offices
Station Road
Brigg
South Humberside DN20 8EG
0652 52441

Hartlepool

Industrial Development Officer
Civic Centre
Hartlepool
Cleveland TS24 8AY
0429 66522

Invergordon

Invergordon Enterprise Zone Office
62 High Street
Invergordon IV18 0DH
0349 853666

Isle of Dogs

London Dockland's Development
Corporation
West India House
Millwall Dock
London E14 9TJ
01-515 3000

Londonderry

Londonderry Enterprise Zone
Office
3 Water Street
Londonderry
0504 263992

Lower Swansea Valley

Director of Planning
Swansea City Council
Guildhall
Swansea SA1 4NL
0792 50821

Middlesbrough

Enterprise Zone Office
Vancouver House
Gurney Street
Middlesbrough
Cleveland TS1 1QP
0642 222279

Milford Haven

Preseli District Council
Cambria House
PO Box 27
Haverfordwest
Dyfed SA61 1TP
0437 4551

North East Lancashire

NE Lancs Development Association
Stephen House
Bethesda Street
Burnley
Lancashire BB11 1PR
0282 37411

North West Kent

NW Kent Enterprise Office
Mountbatten House
3 Military Road
Chatham
Kent ME4 4JE
0634 826233

Rotherham

Rotherham Metropolitan District
Council
Department of Planning
Norfolk House
Walker Place
Rotherham
South Yorkshire S60 1QT
0709 72099

Salford

Industrial Liaison Officer
City of Salford
Civic Centre
Chorley Road
Swinton
Greater Manchester M27 2AD
061-793 3237

Scunthorpe

Civic Centre
Ashby Road
Scunthorpe
South Humberside DN16 1AB
0724 862141

Speke

Senior Assistant Secretary
City Solicitors Department
Liverpool City Council
Room 201
Municipal Buildings
Dale Street
Liverpool L69 2DH
051-227 3911

Tayside

Director of Planning
Angus District Council
County Buildings
Forfar DD8 3LG
0307 65101

Telford

Enterprise Zone Manager
Hazeldine House
Central Square
Telford Centre
Telford
0952 502277

Trafford

Industrial Development Officer
Trafford Metropolitan Borough
Council
Town Hall
Stretford
Greater Manchester M32 0TH
061-872 2101

Tyneside

Central Policy Division
City of Newcastle upon Tyne
Civic Centre
Newcastle upon Tyne NE99 2BH
0632 328520

Gateshead Metropolitan Borough
Council
Town Hall
Gateshead
Tyne and Wear NE8 1BP
0632 771011

Wakefield

Planning Department
City of Wakefield District Council
Newton Bar
Wakefield
West Yorkshire WF1 2TT
0924 370211

Wellingborough

Director of Development
Wellingborough Borough Council
Council Offices
Tithe Barn Road
Wellingborough
Northants NN8 1BN
0933 229777

Workington

Enterprise Zone Manager
Allerdale District Council
Holmewood
Cockermouth
Cumbria CA13 0DW
0900 65656

Index